EIGHTH EDITION

OFF THE BEATEN PATH®
SOUTH CAROLINA ➡

A GUIDE TO UNIQUE PLACES

WILLIAM PRICE FOX

REVISED & UPDATED BY
LEE DAVIS PERRY

gpp®
travel

Guilford, Connecticut

All the information in this guidebook is subject to change. We recommend that you call ahead to obtain current information before traveling.

To buy books in quantity for corporate use
or incentives, call **(800) 962-0973**
or e-mail **premiums@GlobePequot.com.**

Editor: Amy Lyons
Project Editor: Lauren Brancato
Text Design: Linda R. Loiewski
Layout: Joanna Beyer
Maps: Equator Graphics © Morris Book Publishing, LLC

ISSN 1545-5130
ISBN 978-0-7627-7327-5

Printed in the United States of America

10 9 8 7 6 5 4 3 2 1

CLIP AND SAVE:
REAL SIMPLE TO GO

---

trust the experts

A roundup of this issue's smartest tips, courtesy of *Real Simple*'s editors and go-to sources.

LIFE BALANCE

It's possible to train yourself to be more patient. One way is to choose an activity that you do often (taking a sip of water, touching a door handle), then think of the word *patience* every time you do it. Repeat every day for a week and you'll start to feel calmer.

—*Allan Lokos, founder of the Community Meditation Center, in New York City*

BEAUTY

If you're hitting the road this summer, you want your makeup to arrive with you all in one piece. Try this little trick: Stick a cotton ball or pad in a powder compact to act as a buffer between the color and the case. It will keep the powder from crumbling en route.

—*Michelle Phan, cocreator of Em cosmetics*

ORGANIZING

You can never have enough trays at home. Get them in different sizes and colors to use on your nightstand, on a coffee table for remotes and *objets,* or on a desk as a landing spot for office tools, like a stapler and a pen cup. On pretty trays, assorted items look purposeful and neat.

—*Beth Zeigler, Los Angeles–based organizer and blogger at bneato.com*

FOOD

Miso, a flavor-packed staple of Asian cooking used to add richness and depth to soups and dips, is worth keeping on hand. Store an open container, covered, in the refrigerator for up to a year. Or store it in the freezer, where it will keep almost indefinitely. Let it thaw for about an hour before use.

—*Chris Morocco, Real Simple staff food editor*

---

strawberry mixology
MAKE ALL THESE FUN (AND FRUITY) COCKTAILS IN UNDER 5 MINUTES.

VODKA SPRITZER
Combine 4 sliced **strawberries**, 1 **orange wedge**, and 2 ounces **vodka** in a highball glass. Top with **ice** and **seltzer**.

GINGER MARGARITA
Puree 15 hulled **strawberries**, 1 teaspoon grated **fresh ginger**, 2 ounces **tequila**, 2 tablespoons **lime juice**, and 1½ cups **ice** in a blender. Serve with a **lime wedge**.

ELDERFLOWER COCKTAIL
Muddle 4 **strawberries**, 1 teaspoon **sugar**, and 1 strip **lemon peel** in a shaker. Add 2 ounces **gin**, 2 ounces **elderflower liqueur**, 2 tablespoons **lemon juice**, and **ice** and shake.

BOURBON JULEP
Muddle 4 hulled **strawberries** and 2 tablespoons **mint leaves** in a glass. Top with 2 ounces **bourbon** and **crushed ice**. Serve with a **mint sprig**.

CLIP AND SAVE:
REAL SIMPLE TO GO

ILLUSTRATION BY RYO TAKEMASA

COCKTAIL RECIPES

PHOTOGRAPH BY LEVI BROWN

Contents

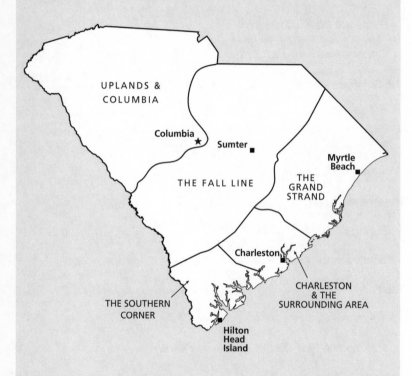

UPLANDS &
COLUMBIA

Columbia ★ Sumter ■

THE FALL LINE

Myrtle
Beach ■

THE
GRAND
STRAND

Charleston ■

CHARLESTON
& THE
SURROUNDING AREA

THE SOUTHERN
CORNER

Hilton
Head
Island

About the Authors

William Price Fox grew up in the Low Country of South Carolina. He has worked as a salesman in New York, a scriptwriter in Hollywood, and a professor at the Writer's Workshop at the University of Iowa. He is the author of seven novels and short story collections, including *Southern Fried Plus Six, Ruby Red, Chitlin Strut & Other Madrigals,* and *Wild Blue Yonder.* His latest book is *Satchel Paige's America,* from the University of Alabama Press. His articles and short stories have been published in magazines and newspapers such as *Sports Illustrated, Travel & Leisure, Golf Digest, Esquire, The Saturday Evening Post,* and the *Los Angeles Times.* A movie has been made based on his stories, *108 Stitches.* He was the producer and moderator of the University of South Carolina E.T.V. Writer's Workshop Program and lives in Columbia.

Lee Davis Perry was born in Greenville, raised in Charleston, and now spends most of her time in the Midlands on Lake Murray—making her an all-around South Carolinian through and through. Lee earned a journalism degree from the University of Georgia in 1976, working in Atlanta advertising agencies, including J. Walter Thompson, following graduation. Her freelance work as an advertising consultant has captured national marketing awards, and her writing has found its way into regional and national magazines. Lee is the author of the book *More Than Petticoats: Remarkable South Carolina Women* and has also coauthored *It Happened in South Carolina, South Carolina Curiosities,* and numerous editions of *Insiders' Guide to Charleston,* all for Globe Pequot Press.

Introduction

Right off the bat, let me get you started on your South Carolina travels with a little background on our distinctive state. My dad, who spent some time in Europe during World War II and who could hold the center of the room with the best of them, had his own theory about why South Carolina is so different from the rest of the country. When he was in Palermo, he said, he saw a painting of St. George slaying the dragon in which George was more than 6 feet tall and built like a wide receiver. The dragon came in at around 80 hands high, weighing more than 50 tons and throwing out a 60-foot sheet of blue-red flame. As he traveled north through Italy, Dad kept seeing the same painting, but while George stayed about the same size, the dragon kept losing weight and getting smaller. In Germany he was down to the size of a Clydesdale. Finally, in Copenhagen, Dad couldn't believe his eyes. "That dragon still looked like a dragon, but the artist had shrunk him down to the size of a good-sized rabbit. Old George was holding him up by one ear, and I mean he couldn't have dressed out no more than four pounds, tops."

Then he wrapped it up. "The way I see it, South Carolina is about like Palermo. We have more imagination down here, and you know, bigger visions. You get north, up above Richmond, and it's like Copenhagen."

Along with this rich imagination, we also have the Gullah dialect, which is still heard down in the Low Country and out on the sea islands. Down here they still "read heads" and "work roots." They believe that "haint blue" and "haint green" painted on the doorjambs and window trims will keep the evil spirits away and that if you sweep your yard before the sun comes up, Doctor Death will keep on the other side of the road and go on about his business.

In Gullah, "he" stands for he, she, or it, and "um" stands for it, her, him, or them. Many of the words and phrases run on pure sound and cadence, and with the high-low jackrabbit delivery much of it sounds like calypso. If it sounds good, it is good. Proper names can be name brands, road signs, or a quick and clever riff from a new tune. One woman near Beaufort, who was named during the Kennedy funeral, proudly displays Cathedral Rotunda Johnson above the red birds on her rural delivery mailbox. And over near Fripp Island, the town of Pocotaligo is the compression of "poke a turtle's tail and he will go." Of the translatable Gullah proverbs and bromides, here are a fast few:

"Ef you play wid puppy, ee lick you face." (Familiarity breeds contempt.)

"Ef you ent hab hoss to ride, ride cow." (Half a loaf is better than none.)

"Po buckra an dog walk one pat." (The poor man and the dog walk the same path.)

If South Carolina looks like anything, it's a slice of pie that has not only been badly cut but lifted out of the pan much too early. Starting in the northwest corner at the Chattooga River—about the spot where Sheriff James Dickey, the late poet-in-residence at the University of South Carolina, leaned on his patrol car in the film *Deliverance*—the South Carolina–North Carolina line runs east for 333 rugged miles to Little River and the Atlantic Ocean. From Little River the uninterrupted shoreline, with some of the best beaches in the country, stretches south more than 200 miles to Tybee Sound, only a few miles from Savannah, Georgia. From here up the wide Savannah River back to the northwest corner and the Chattooga, it's 240 miles.

Roughly paralleling the South Carolina coastline and running across the center of the state is another line—the Fall Line. This separates two distinct regions—the Upcountry and the Low Country, with the sandy Midlands in between. Most of the Upcountry is plateaus with rolling hills, ragged woods, fast-moving streams, and red-clay earth. First settled by Germans, Scots-Irish, and Welsh early in the 18th century, by 1800 the Upcountry had more than 30,000 small farmers who, with their self-sufficient way of life, had almost nothing in common with Low Country plantation owners. Today, while this region still has a great deal of farmland that produces soybeans,

explodingafew southcarolina myths

A hoop snake will not put its tail in its mouth and roll down a hill.

A diamondback rattler will not wrap around your leg to hold you still while it bites. Now that would be scary!

A red fox will not run on three legs (resting a fourth) when running from the dogs.

Fire ants will not swarm over your legs and then, on a mysterious signal from their leader, bite you all at once. But don't try this one out. They can be absolutely savage and terrifying, and nothing short of a blowtorch can kill them.

peaches, cotton, and tobacco, it is also a highly successful national and international manufacturing center. The giant BMW plant in Greenville is a notable example.

During the agricultural development of the Upcountry, the merchant-planters of the Low Country were living in the grand style of English gentle-men. Having named their first settlement Charles Town for England's King Charles II—the Merry Monarch who encouraged theater, horse racing, fine dining, dancing, and even golf—they were maintaining beautifully deco-rated town houses as well as sprawling and magnificent plantations and sending their children to London, Edinburgh, and Paris for their education.

Until only a few years ago, on East Bay Street in Charleston, the oldest printers in the South, Walker, Evans and Cogswell, knowing the precari-ous ways of the American dollar, still held onto their original Confederate money plates. Charlestonians are like this. They hold onto anything old: their houses, their furniture, their she-crab soup recipes, and their accents. It's this "holding-on" to the best aspects of the past and the sacred belief in landmarks that make Charleston possibly the most beautiful city in the country. With its low skyline and lantern-lit cobblestone streets, you can stroll along at night with a good domestic wine and a little imagination and find yourself in southern France or Ireland's County Kerry, or, for the more literary, the pages of Jane Austen.

Charlestonians also, despite earthquakes, hurricanes, plagues, and out-right ridicule, cling to their family names with a desperation that approaches that of the American Kennel Club. If a young married lady is introducing herself, she might admit that she is now unfortunately a Hampton. "I'm Elizabeth Moultrie Hampton." Then, with a perfectly sensible "south of Broad Street" change of key, she'll quickly add, "wuzza Heyward," letting you know there were cotillions and better days in the not-too-distant past.

I grew up in the Midlands, 100 miles north of Charleston in Columbia. Every day on the way to school, I could see the green-domed capitol of the State House and the bronze stars on the western side marking the spots where Sherman's shells had struck. They are still there and will probably be there forever. We grew up here with history all around us. In the old section of town, the streets are named for the Revolutionary generals Bull, Sumter, Pickens, and Marion. In the newer sections they bear the names of the Confederates: Lee, Jackson, Longstreet, Hampton, Pickett, and Green. In

South Carolina Food Specialties

- Pimento cheese (Ruth's is the classic and can be found at most grocery stores.)

- Boiled peanuts (Buy raw peanuts, stick them in a TON of water, with a TON of salt, approximately four cups worth, and boil until they look as if they've lost all integrity!)

- Pickled boiled eggs

- Pecan pie/sweet potato pie

- Pepper jelly on cream cheese and crackers

- Pork rinds (These can be bought in any store.)

the section called "The Bottom," the names run the gamut from local politicians and famed prizefighters to attitudes and ambitions: Do Rite Alley, Easy Street, Sugar Ray Robinson Boulevard and Joe Louis Boulevard, and Captain Marvel Road (which is only 80 feet long and dead-ends into a trash pile). Everything else, from bridges and landfills to rest stops and runoff culverts, is named for the late Strom Thurmond.

In the small towns around Columbia, Greenville, and Spartanburg and on up to the North Carolina line, some traditions are set in stone and never change. The Atlantic coastline and the Southern tracks still gleam in the white gravel and the bright sun, and barefoot kids still walk the hot rails in the summertime. Fords, Chevys, and Plymouths, wrapped in honeysuckle and wisteria vines, still rust and rot out in the front yards and down in the drain ditches, and groups of three and four and five dogs still meet for all-night sessions under the streetlights at the crossroads.

We grew up here in the Midlands shooting squirrels in the swamp and carp in the river and rats at the trash pile. We sold iron to the iron man, paper to the paper man, and whiskey bottles to the bootleggers. We rode our bikes down the 50 or 60 or 70 steps of the State House, the courthouse, or whatever wedding-cake building was standing in the town square. We went to school here and joined the service here and came back from the service and went back to school here. Many of us left and went north or west or abroad, but almost all of us came back. Very few of us can put our finger on exactly why. Perhaps the best reason is that while we know it can get hot here in the summertime and pretty cool in the winter, the old Palmetto State is unlike any other place in the world.

Despite Hollywood's thigh-slapping, yee-hawing, chain-saw-dueling portrayal of South Carolinians, there is still a modicum of propriety and politeness down here not often found in the severe latitudes in the north. You will actually see men tip their hats to women and even give them their seats on the bus—there are no subways. And back in the smaller towns, suicides are toned down and usually reported as "after a short illness." But there are a few ground rules that you should know to make your trip here as easy and pleasant as possible.

Grits are served with all breakfasts. You can request home fries, but don't be too surprised at what you get. Your best bet is to butter the grits, add pepper, mix them with your eggs, and not complain. An even better bet is to find a place that serves yellow grits instead of white—more on that later.

And contrary to what you've seen in the movies or read in the *National Enquirer,* there are no radar traps that track only northern license plates. The Highway Patrol officers are extremely helpful. If you have a flat tire or engine trouble, just sit back and wait. They'll come along and make all the

South Carolina Facts

- South Carolina was the eighth state to sign the Constitution and the first state to secede from the Union before the Civil War. Edisto Island, south of Charleston, decreed that if the state didn't secede, it would secede from South Carolina.

- South Carolina grows more peaches than any other state except California.

- South Carolina has one of the oldest formal gardens in America—the Gardens at Middleton Place, created in 1741.

- South Carolina has 187 miles of coastline and arguably the best beaches in America. On some beaches you won't see a single soul for more than a mile, even in the middle of summer.

- On a hot day, kudzu can grow more than a foot. Some teachers string it across the outside of a window so the pupils can actually watch it grow.

arrangements for towing, tire changing, and so on. As a matter of fact, most of the Highway Patrol's time is spent doing precisely this. Many of them are very good shade-tree mechanics.

In the Low Country be careful driving during a heavy rainstorm. Especially in downtown Charleston, often the rain will come with a high tide, and the lower streets will flood with a mix of fresh and salt water that can ruin your car in minutes. Do not try to drive through this. Sit still until the water recedes, or leave the car and come back for it later, when it dries out.

Due to the fact that South Carolina has been one of the poorest states for so many years, the federal government has stepped in and built an excellent highway system. The four interstates—I-20, I-77, I-26, and I-95—that crisscross the state may very well be the best and smoothest in the country. We also have well-equipped and beautifully maintained rest stops. And like most of the rest of the country, you can turn right on a red light.

Sunday blue laws are too complicated to discuss in detail. Basically they assume that we all should be in church on Sunday and have no business shopping, drinking, or browsing through the malls from 8 a.m. to noon. Each county has its own laws, but most of them are now allowing stores, movies, and malls to open after noon. While you cannot buy beer or wine on Sunday, bars that have paid a stiff Sunday sales tax can be open on Sunday nights until midnight. All this will vary from county to county. Another blue law, called the Sundown Law, stipulates that you can't buy liquor from a package store after the sun goes down. This law is in effect every night of the week. You can, however, buy wine and beer from almost any store.

A very helpful resource is the Parks, Recreation, and Tourism Department. Their phone number is (803) 734-1700 or (866) 224-9339, and they're open from 8 a.m. to 5 p.m. Mon through Fri. They can be contacted for free brochures and any and all information. Their website is scprt.com.

In South Carolina, everything happens on Labor Day. The football season opens, and in this part of the country, that's a religious experience in its own right. Across the sandhills and the Piedmont and on down the Congaree and the Cooper Rivers to Charleston, more than 100 official barbecues, okra struts, catfish stomps, and demolition derbies all crank up at the same time. How to choose the best one is hard. But they're out there and all you have to do is check the papers or call the chambers of commerce.

South Carolina State Symbols

State Tree—Palmetto Tree

State Nickname—The Palmetto State

State Animal—White-tailed Deer

State Game Bird—Wild Turkey

State Fish—Striped Bass

State Reptile—Loggerhead Turtle

State Insect—Carolina Mantid

State Butterfly—Eastern Tiger Swallowtail

State Dog—Boykin Spaniel

State Bird—Carolina Wren

State Flower—Yellow Jessamine

State Motto—"Prepared in mind and resources. While I breathe, I hope."

Part of living in South Carolina and celebrating the survival of summer is the fall and the hundred fairs that crowd the calendars of the chambers of commerce. There are county fairs, town fairs, and fairs jimmied up at the crossroads with sawhorse tables for the pies and pickle relishes and rides that fold down from the backs of pickup trucks. The big one, the State Fair, is in Columbia in mid-October, and swirling around the centerpiece—a Saturn Rocket shipped up from Cape Canaveral—are more than 100,000 locals and not-so-locals eating elephant's ears, fried pies, and corn dogs, and then settling down to a first-class home-cooked meal in their favorite church tent while their kids ride everything from the Bumble Bee—for two-year-olds—to the Zipper, which after 30 years or so only the very young and the very drunk still ride.

South Carolina, with its own language, customs, and rhythms, is different. Very different. You'll see glimpses of it down on the coast in the shrimp boats and the oyster boats heading out at dawn and coming back in at dusk. You'll see it in the great blue heron as it glides across a marsh and settles under a moss-draped cypress tree, or in the possum—the small dog that doesn't bark—crossing a road carrying her litter. And you'll see it in that soft and sliding light at first dark that turns the roofs of Charleston from red to orange to gold to umber.

I guess my dad was probably right; if we're like anything, we're like Palermo because, while we know that much of what we carry on about doesn't make a helluva lot of sense, we believe it anyway. In short, we have our own vision and version of history that works like this: It could have been, it should have been, it was. And in this happy delusion—sustained by azaleas in January and February, magnolias from March to August, gardenias, roses, wisteria, and 20-foot-high banana trees, fresh shrimp, and weather you can play golf in almost every day of the year—we still believe if Lee had had Jackson on his flank at Gettysburg, we could have won the day and the war, and the capital of these United States would be dead-center between Greenville 100 miles north and Charleston 100 miles south, right here in Columbia where it was originally scheduled to be. We also believe what one of our leaders proclaimed years ago: that while South Carolina is too small for a good-sized plantation and too big for an insane asylum, it's the only state in the nation that doesn't envy Virginia.

H. L. Mencken, no slouch with superlatives, went one better when he called the South Carolina lifestyle "a civilization of manifold excellences, perhaps the best the Western Hemisphere has ever seen."

That's pretty much the story on South Carolina from where I sit. These are some of the basic truths, anyway. I hope you enjoy yourself while traveling here in the Palmetto State. I really enjoyed putting this guidebook together on your behalf. But you need to be forewarned about something—South Carolina tends to grow on folks. They tend to swing back through here sooner rather than later when they start getting the wanderlust.

Here's to new adventures and the sweet, open road.

CHARLESTON & THE SURROUNDING AREA

Downtown Charleston

Are you ready to immerse yourself in the crown jewel of South Carolina? *Charleston*—which has been called The Holy City; The City by the Sea, Where the Ashley and the Cooper Rivers Meet to Form the Atlantic Ocean; and The Home of Rhett Butler—is the perfect place to begin a tour of the old Palmetto State. Settled in 1670, this remarkable town literally has to be seen to be believed.

My grandmother, who was from the Midlands around Columbia, used to huff and hiss, "Charlestonians are all right but everybody knows they're just too poor to paint and too proud to whitewash." That used to be true. Not anymore. One look at the real estate prices, and you'll see how much that's all changed.

You might consider seriously the recommendation that you don't even think about driving around Charleston. The streets are narrow, some are paved with cobblestones, and the one-way traffic can be a nightmare in rush hours. (Women wearing high heels will have a tough time negotiating cobblestones.) Parking on the street is almost

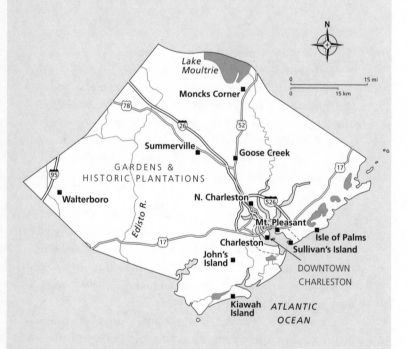

impossible. The easier approach is to park your car in a downtown lot or the visitor center and forget it. The standard rate is about $10 a day.

Since Charleston and the Low Country area attract more than four million guests each year, hotel, guest house, and bed-and-breakfast owners have built a reputation for hospitality and extremely high standards. Charleston is famous for its bed-and-breakfasts in particular, and one local service does everything possible to match the guests to whatever sort of accommodations they want: *Historic Charleston Bed and Breakfast* (843-722-6606 or 800-743-3583; historiccharlestonbedandbreakfast.com).

Some bed-and-breakfasts provide bicycles that will help you get around the city on tours of your own arrangement. Lodgings in these homes and inns provide the wonderful feeling that you are staying in the very heart of the old city like a true Charlestonian. Listed below are a few that are off the beaten path yet have all the amenities for an enjoyable, comfortable stay.

At *Battery Carriage House Inn,* 20 South Battery, rates range from $180 to $299 and include continental breakfast, wine and cheese in the evening, and turn-down service. The majority of the rooms are off a side garden but you're steps away from Charleston's famous Battery and White Point Gardens. The rooms are furnished in period reproductions. Each room has its own private bath as well as separate air-conditioning and heating controls. Call (843) 727-3100 or (800) 775-5575, or visit batterycarriage house.com.

Lowndes Grove Plantation, 266 Margaret St., offers a unique accommodation experience that's clearly off the beaten path from the Battery, as mentioned above. Yet this is an authentic Ashley River plantation house and one that's actually within the city limits. The house, built about 1786, and its landscaped grounds give guests a rural feeling of open space, spectacular gardens, and fabulous views of the historic river itself. This house once hosted President Theodore Roosevelt when it was part of the 1901 West Indies Exhibition at nearby Hampton Park. Three air-conditioned guest suites in the main house plus a two-room guest cottage (priced from $175 to $200) all have enormous antebellum charm. Call (843) 853-1810 or visit pphgcharleston.com.

Here's how you might begin a Charleston tour. Make *The Mills House* on the corner of Meeting and Queen your starting point. It's located in the very center of the old town. Then try a walking tour of a

TOP RECOMMENDATIONS IN CHARLESTON & THE SURROUNDING AREA

Angel Oak
3688 Angel Oak Rd.
Johns Island
(843) 559-3496

The Battery
At the tip of the Charleston peninsula

Best Friend Bar at The Mills House
115 Meeting St.
(843) 577-2400
millshouse.com

Boone Hall
1235 Long Point Rd.
Mt. Pleasant
(843) 884-4371
boonehallplantation.com

The Calhoun Mansion
16 Meeting St.
(843) 722-8205
calhounmansion.net

Charleston Country Club
1 Country Club Dr.
(843) 795-0422
countryclubofcharleston.com

Dock Street Theatre
135 Church St.
(843) 720-3968
charlestonstage.com

Middleton Place
4300 Ashley River Rd.
(843) 556-6020 or (800) 782-3608
middletonplace.org

Ocean Course at Kiawah
(843) 768-2121 or (800) 654-2924
kiawahisland.com

St. Michael's Episcopal Church
Corner of Meeting and Broad Streets
(843) 723-0603
stmichaelschurch.net

few spots nearby. Several tours depart from there or close by. Or, you can go it alone following this guide. If you can, spend a night or two at The Mills House. It's a beautiful restoration of what it was before the Civil War. As a matter of fact, on the second floor you can stand on the wrought-iron balcony where in 1861 Robert E. Lee stood and watched much of the old town burn.

The 214-room hotel is located at 115 Meeting St. and has accommodations that range from $150 to suites up to $550; adjacent parking is available at an extra charge. It has an outdoor swimming pool on the third floor with a very comfortable sundeck where you can get a cool drink and a light snack. The **_Best Friend Bar_** on the lobby floor, with very good local musical talent, is the perfect spot after a night on the town. Across the beautiful marble lobby is the recently refurbished **_Barbados Room,_** which has earned the

Mobil Travel Guide four-star award. Here they serve breakfast, lunch, and a romantic candlelit dinner. The evening menu is expensive, but worth it. The Sunday brunch there is fantastic. Before you dine, be sure to sip a drink in the fountain courtyard. For reservations and information, call (843) 577-2400 or visit millshouse.com.

Still using The Mills House as a starting point, you can cross Meeting and walk exactly one block down Queen to Church to one of the oldest and most charming operating playhouses in the country, the **Dock Street Theatre.** The original theater, built in 1735, has long vanished, but the 1800s hotel built on the site was converted into a theater in 1935, by the Works Progress Administration (WPA). During Spoleto, the 17-day annual music and art festival held in Charleston in late May and early June, the theater is the centerpiece for chamber music and plays. A few years back, one of Arthur Miller's last plays premiered here.

The Dock Street Theatre completed a major face-lift in 2010, and you might catch it open for tours and individual browsing from 10 a.m. to 4 p.m. Mon through Fri unless a rehearsal is under way. The building, which has been reconstructed over and over again, handsomely captures the Georgian architecture that flourished during that period. Dock Street seats 463 and has a pit and a parquet of 13 boxes. Over the stage is a carved wood bas-relief of the Royal Coat of Arms of England. The cove ceiling has exceptional acoustic properties—when string quartets perform here during the Spoleto Festival, any seat in the house is a good seat.

The old theater plays a leading role in the intellectual and cultural life of the city. All year long the theater features dramas, musicals, and family fare, as well as readings and recitals. Late May and early June are booked solid with concerts and plays during the Spoleto Festival. Call (843) 720-3968 for information or visit charlestonstage.com.

A block and a half back up Queen and past The Mills House is **82 Queen,** a combination oyster bar, stand-up brass-railed pub, and fine restaurant. The building, formerly two adjoining 19th-century town houses, has a lovely courtyard dining area complete with awnings, umbrellas, and banks of shrubbery. Specialties here are seafood, beef, and fowl, with prices ranging from $12 to $28. The bar, which fronts on Queen, is a notorious hangout for local authorities on everything from ornithology to transcendentalism, and if you listen long enough you will probably hear it all. One local sage, deep in the grape, cornered me not too long ago with the red-hot, ice-cold information that Charleston inbreeding, which rivals that of the ancient Egyptians, has been going on so long and with such intensity that there isn't an empty attic on the whole peninsula. Call (843) 722-4428 or go to 82queen.com.

A few doors back up Queen at number 72 is **Poogan's Porch,** which serves gumbos, jambalayas, and great crab cakes. The bread pudding and peanut butter pie are especially good and have become a tradition here on Queen. You can eat indoors or out on the veranda. For lunch, stay inside with the air-conditioning. For dinner, when it cools off, it's nice to eat out-side. The name Poogan came from the dog who was left behind when the original owner sold the house and moved away. Since then the restaurant has changed hands several times, but each time the dog remained behind as the mascot until he died in 1979. Poogan's is open every day for lunch and dinner. Prices range from $10 to $28. Call (843) 577-2337 or check out poogansporch.com.

From Poogan's Porch go back to The Mills House and follow Meeting Street south to 38 Tradd St. Turn left here and walk one block to 38 Tradd St. This was the home of the painter Elizabeth O'Neill Verner (1883–1979), internationally famous for her pen-and-ink drawings and paintings of the Charleston skyline, its churches, and the local flower ladies and basket weavers. Prints of her work are on exhibit and for sale exclusively at the **Gibbes Museum of Art gift shop** at 135 Meeting St., just north of The Mills House. Verner's drawings and paintings are quintessentially Charleston and are not to be missed.

Near 38 Tradd St. at 91 Church St. is **Cabbage Row.** Originally four or five connected buildings around a central courtyard, today it is a shop featuring art, antique maps and prints. It was here that Porgy of DuBose Heyward's book of that name lived. "Cabbage Row" was changed to "Cat-fish Row" for DuBose Heyward and George Gershwin's folk opera *Porgy and Bess.* In 1934 Gershwin spent a summer in Charleston and lived a few miles away on Folly Beach, where he and Heyward collaborated on the now world-famous opera set in Charleston. Most of the staging was based on the courtyard, and much of Gershwin's inspiration for the score came from the sounds of the neighborhood street vendors (the strawberry man, the butter bean man, and the fresh shrimp man).

Many of Gershwin's letters to his brother Ira in New York describe life in Charleston in the 1930s and the devastation he witnessed from a hurricane. They also reveal a curious downside to the famous composer. Gershwin, hell-bent on self-promotion, tried to get the Charlestonians to rename Folly Beach as Gershwin Island. Fortunately Charlestonians knew where to draw the line, and Folly Beach is still Folly Beach. These letters are available for reading in the South Carolina room of the **Charleston County Public Library** at 68 Calhoun St.

If you're a football, baseball, basketball, or golf fan and can't stand missing too much of the action, make a note of the **Charleston Crab House** at 41 S. Market St. A wide variety of sandwiches and beverages is available here with a large TV screen carrying all the sports action. Prices are $8 to $15. Call (843) 853-2900 or visit charlestoncrabhouse.com.

On King Street about a block from The Mills House is one of the most elegant and tasteful women's clothing shops on the entire East Coast. Its name, **R.T.W.,** means ready-to-wear, and the place and the selections will make you ready to buy. Once you've tried something on and closed your eyes to the price, you'll probably want to wear it right then and there.

Jan McMenamin is the owner, and she has a marvelous eye for fashion and what particular women need to match their skin tone, eyes, hair, and anything else that needs matching. As a matter of fact, she often goes abroad for a small group of her favorite customers and buys whatever she sees that she knows will please them. She is seldom, if ever, wrong. If you're in a quandary about what you should wear and how you should wear it, see her. For the nervous spouse fingering his credit card, Jan serves complimentary wine, brandy, coffee, tea, and an assortment of local sweets. You can park at the side of the store or one block away at the city parking lot right behind

boiledpeanuts

Look for and buy a sack of boiled peanuts, then see what happens. At first you will be repulsed by their appearance—they're brown and soft and look very, very suspicious. But get over it and try three or four. By the fourth or fifth, you will be hooked for life, and when you head back north you'll be loaded down with them. Unfortunately, like South Carolina peaches and sweet corn, they don't travel well and have to be shelled and eaten as close to the patch as you can get. You can buy them right on the street.

The Mills House. Even if you don't buy anything, go in and look around—it's a one of a kind. Call (843) 577-9748 or check out rtwcharleston.com.

Charleston Place, located at 205 Meeting St., is one of the premier hotels in the South. Off the beautiful lobby is a small but fine selection of stores including St. John, Godiva, Brookstone, Gucci, and Tommy Bahama. The lounge at the hotel is elegant, and while the musicians who play there change frequently, they are all very, very good. Room rates begin at about $200. Call (843) 722-4900 or go to charlestonplacehotel.com.

Nestled within the Shops at Charleston Place, the ***Charleston Grill*** is one of the top dining experiences in town. Break out the fancy duds and resurrect your best table manners, then spend a fine evening trying new fare like octopus salad and poached duck egg or more traditional entrees like the grilled Kurobuta pork chop with basil-creamed corn, tomato coulis, Anson Mills grits, and peach glaze. Wine pairings are suggested for each appetizer and entree, or the sommelier is at hand with more. If you can't decide on dinner, Chef Michelle Weaver offers a six-course tasting menu for your entire table. As you would expect, the service here is impeccable and the ambience lovely and inviting. And the perfect meal wouldn't be perfect without the perfect music to accompany it. They have this covered, too, with world-class jazz seven nights a week. Dinners range from $30 to $50 and up. Their cozy, sophisticated bar opens at 5 p.m. and dinner is served from 5:30 p.m. to 10 p.m. every night. Call (843) 577-4522 for reservations or make them online at charlestongrill.com. It's not altogether "off the beaten path," but it's a place where you should at least drop in for a glass of something.

On the other hand, if really casual is your style, stop by ***Hyman's Seafood*** at 215 Meeting St. next to Charleston Place. It has been voted the number one seafood restaurant in town. They serve 15 to 25 different fish any way you like, as well as shellfish, aged beef, and several pasta dishes. Hyman's specializes in frying with olive oil, and their seafood can be had broiled, fried, or blackened. The okra soup is especially delicious and different. They're open seven days a week from 11 a.m. to 9:30 p.m. Prices range from $5 to $29. If you're driving, which you shouldn't be, park in the Charleston Place garage next door. Call (843) 723-6000 or visit hyman seafood.com.

The Calhoun Mansion at 16 Meeting St. is much more than a house, and a tour of this extravaganza is well worth the price of admission. To begin, it is 24,000 square feet (the average family home is approximately 3,000 square feet). Built in 1876, this privately owned Victorian showplace is divided into 35 rooms, each with different and elaborate tile floors and ornamental plaster molding. The ballroom, with its skylight and 45-foot-high ceiling, is the centerpiece. The furnishings and artwork are eclectic and as unusual as the house itself. For instance, on the second floor is a great surprise for the children—a 14-foot stuffed and rampaging polar bear. One of the best-known movie-making secrets is the fact that the Calhoun Mansion was featured in the television miniseries *North and South* as the Pennsylvania home of the Hazzards. If you meet the right people at 82 Queen or The Best Friend Bar at The Mills House, you might get a sunset tour of the roof of the old mansion, which may be the most beautiful view in all of Charleston. Generally tours are 11 a.m. to 5 p.m., but check for seasonal hours. Admission is $15 per person (more for the whole house and cupola tour); children under 6 are admitted free. Call (843) 722-8205 or visit calhoun mansion.net.

After leaving the Calhoun Mansion, stroll up to the corner of Meeting and Broad, a junction known as the *Four Corners of Law.* Here you'll see the flower ladies, whom Elizabeth O'Neill Verner so lovingly painted, selling daisies, daffodils, or whatever is in season. Most of them are also basket ladies. If you're lucky, you'll hear them singing as they weave their ancient patterns from sweetgrass, pine needles, and bulrushes and bind their elaborate work together with fiber strips from palmetto trees. The baskets, which come in a variety of shapes and sizes, are truly unique and can be purchased here and out on Highway 17 heading north toward Mt. Pleasant. They last for generations and make wonderful presents.

After this little excursion, which should give you a feeling for the old town, your next best stop is the *Charleston Visitor Reception and Transportation Center* at 375 Meeting St. One of the best visitor centers in the country, it can save you time, money, and especially shoe leather if you decide to go on the walking tours. Its gracious and well-informed attendants can help you with almost everything, including tours, lodging, restaurants, parking, attractions, and entertainment.

Built in 1856, the visitor center is a redbrick, high-ceilinged building that was formerly the Railroad Depot. Large-scale maps along with old photos and prints illustrate how the city has changed and developed since 1670, when the first English settlers anchored here and came ashore. Computerized maps equipped with video stations are also available. You can call up information on interactive screens and request additional advice on direct-line telephones. A service counter with helpful attendants is at your disposal and is a central location for obtaining tour and theater tickets.

A 20-minute show entitled *Forever Charleston* is a combination of slides, music, city sounds, and narration by Charlestonians. Shown every half hour, it is a beautifully photographed production but seems long on charm and short on story, insight, and humor. It also needs a cleaner sound track. Nonetheless, buy a couple of pecan pralines from the attendant—they are delicious—and see it anyway. The tidewater panoramas and heron, egret, and alligator shots are worth the $2 admission and will get you in the perfect mood for touring the incredible homes, gardens, and plantations around the old city. The center is open from 8:30 a.m. to 5:30 p.m. daily but closes a half hour earlier in Nov, Dec, Jan, and Feb. It is also closed on Thanksgiving, Christmas, and New Year's Day. Call (843) 853-8000 or (800) 868-8118, or go to charlestoncvb.com.

Next door to the visitor center, you'll find a depot for the ***Downtown Area Shuttles (DASH),*** which leave every 15 minutes for tours through different sections of Charleston. DASH shuttles for tourists are the green "trolleys," different from the CARTA mass-transit buses. And riding DASH is free! A good bet is to take several rides so you can figure out what area of town you'd like to explore by foot or horse-drawn carriage ride. Many people make the DASH depot their first stop, parking their cars here and taking a few quick rides in the shuttles before deciding where they would like to stay. For more on DASH and CARTA, go to ridecarta.com.

If you head back toward The Mills House Hotel from the visitor center along Meeting Street, you'll find yourself approaching the white brick Days Inn motel on the right at 155 Meeting St. What would otherwise be the motel's rather expected restaurant, attached to the complex just off the parking lot, is actually an independent eatery called ***Toast.*** Well, Toast is anything but expected. In fact, this may be one of the best-kept secrets in Charleston. The food is relatively inexpensive, as the peninsula restaurants go, and that's your first break. Then, the portions are enormous and the cooking is truly fine. If you're anywhere near here at breakfast time, you must try the apple French toast. The Crab Cake Sammie is a delight for lunch, and there's an array of dinner specials every night. The dessert kiosk filled with pies and cakes is beyond temptation. They even have a small cocktail bar for "happy hour" or a cold beer on a hot day. Toast opens at 6 a.m. for those who want to get an early start on discovering Charleston. Dinner reservations are suggested, as the seating is limited and Toast's secret is getting out. Call (843) 534-0043, visit toastofcharleston.com, or check out the list of specials posted on the chalkboard outside.

From Toast, it's only a block farther south to the ***Gibbes Museum of Art*** at 135 Meeting St. Considered one of the best collections in the entire Southeast, this museum exhibits 500 18th- and 19th-century portraits and paintings as well as sculptures and Japanese wood-block prints. The gift shop has a wonderful collection of note cards, postcards, and books that make excellent gifts. Don't be afraid to bring the kids here; there is plenty to keep them amused and busy. Open Tues through Sat from 10 a.m. to 5 p.m. and Sun 1 to 5 p.m.; closed Mon. Admission is $9 for adults, $7 for seniors and college students, and $5 for children ages 6 to 12. Call (843) 722-2706 or visit gibbesmuseum.org.

For the budget minded, only a few blocks away—we're still walking— you'll find ***Jestine's Kitchen*** at 251 Meeting St. The specialties here are Low Country home cooking, vegetables, fish, and really wonderful fried chicken. The price range is from $7 to $15. Open from 11 a.m. to 9:30 p.m. Tues through Thurs, 11 a.m. to 10 p.m. Fri and Sat, and 11 a.m. to 9 p.m. Sun; closed Mon. Call (843) 722-7224.

On the other hand, you can go to ***S.N.O.B.*** at 192 E. Bay St. for exquisite dining and an equally exquisite atmosphere. The tongue-in-cheek acronym officially stands for its location, "Slightly North of Broad." The specialty here is Low Country cooking along with a number of very fine continental dishes. One of the local favorites is shrimp and yellow grits. Prices range from $12 to $32, and wine is served. Lunch is served from 11:30 a.m. to 3 p.m., dinner from 5:30 to 10 p.m. While down south, try to get yellow grits rather than white. There's a big, big difference—the yellow are not overprocessed and have a much better taste. You can even buy them, although only in some stores. Call S.N.O.B. at (843) 723-3424 or visit slightlynorthofbroad.net.

On up the street from The Mills House is the ***Joseph Manigault House*** at 350 Meeting St. This classic example of the elegant Adam style was designed and built by the architect Gabriel Manigault for his brother,

Joseph, in 1803. The graceful, elliptical staircase, which you will also see in the *Forever Charleston* show back at the visitor center, is the centerpiece. In the 1920s the place was a broken-down boardinghouse, and for a while in the 1930s it was a service station. The dean of the Harvard School of Architecture and a number of Charlestonians took it upon themselves to help restore and furnish it with the period furniture you see here today. This is one of the few houses in Charleston that still has a gatehouse. Open 10 a.m. to 5 p.m. Mon through Sat and 1 to 5 p.m. Sun (closed on major holidays). Last tour is at 4:30 p.m. Admission is $10 for adults and $5 for children 3 to 12. Contact the Charleston Museum at (843) 722-2996 for combination tickets to all of their museum sites. Their website is charleston museum.org.

For one of the best views with a little sea breeze to boot, you simply have to visit the **Rooftop Terrace Bar at Vendue Inn,** located at 19 Vendue Range. This popular spot offers a charming view of the churches and many of the old tile roofs and quaint chimneys of the old city, with glimpses of Charleston Harbor. The cuisine here is focused on seafood and other light fare, and they offer a nice variety of specialty drinks that give you that vacation feeling. Prices are around $7 to $22. Call (843) 577-7970 or (800) 845-7900. Open seven days a week from 11:30 in the morning to midnight. Visit vendueinn.com.

The **Nathaniel Russell House,** located at 51 Meeting St., is another showcase home and a Charleston favorite. Spacious gardens surround this old house, recognized as one of America's finest examples of neoclassical architecture. Its elaborate plasterwork ornamentation, its free-flying staircase rising up through three complete stories without any visible means of support, and its beautiful proportions prompted the celebrated French aristocrat Henry Deas Lesesne to proclaim it to be "beyond all comparison the finest establishment in Charleston." Open Mon through Sat from 10 a.m. to 5 p.m. and Sun 2 to 5 p.m. Admission is $10 for adults and $5 for children 6 to 16; younger than 6 are admitted free. Call (843) 724-8481 or go to historic charleston.org.

Lodge Alley at 195 E. Bay St. is a place that anyone who has the slightest interest in renovation shouldn't miss. A dozen years ago this was an ugly string of decaying warehouses. Today it is a beautiful inn with a fountain in the center court and an excellent restaurant next door called **High Cotton.**

The specialties at the restaurant are roast squab and rack of lamb, as well as seafood and Low Country cuisine. If you don't stay here or eat here, at least stop by for a drink at the small, intimate bar overlooking the courtyard, but beware of time-share salespeople lurking about. Call (843) 722-1611 or visit bluegreenrentals.com.

Gaulart and Maliclet at 98 Broad St., in the heart of the city, prides itself on being fast and French. They are just that—and given the high quality of their food and fine service, surprisingly economical. I had a cup of delicious split-pea soup, a sandwich of pâté and blue cheese, and excellent coffee for around $6. They have a very fine wine list, but best of all, their steady customers all seem remarkably upbeat and happy and seem to know one another. This is one of the smallest eateries in town, but it's also one of the really very fine Charleston surprises. It's a great place to drop in for breakfast, lunch, or dinner and sit at the bar and listen to the music and the local gossip. Open 8 a.m. to 4 p.m. Mon, 8 a.m. to 10 p.m. Tues through Thurs, and 8 a.m. to 10:30 p.m. Fri and Sat. Call (843) 577-9797 or see fast andfrenchcharleston.com.

Of course, no visit to Charleston would be complete without a trip to **The Battery.** But first a little background on the site. This tip of the Charleston peninsula was first called White Point Garden due to the white expanse of sand and the bleached oyster shells that identified it as a prominent marker when the colonists were settling the area in 1670. The point later gained fame in 1718 when Stede Bonnet and 19 of his fellow pirates "took

Summers in Paris

One of the better walking-around stories down here about Charleston concerns an elderly pair of sisters who had fallen on lean times. Despite their circumstances they insisted on telling everyone that nothing had changed and they were still summering in Paris. At night, when the rest of the town was asleep, they would slip out of their shuttered house and take their constitutional along The Battery. One night a child recognized them and wanted to say hello. Her mother held her back, saying, "No, dear, we don't speak to them in the summertime. They're still in Paris."

If this isn't the story that made Charleston "the most civilized town in the country," it certainly should be.

the air" here with ropes around their necks, an event that brought an end to the coastal piracy that had plagued the nearby waters.

On April 12, 1861, Charlestonians sought vantage points here to watch the Confederate guns fire on the Union troops stationed at Fort Sumter. The cheers went up, Rhett Butler groaned (fictionally, years later in Margaret Mitchell's *Gone with the Wind*), and the Civil War had started. When Union forces left Fort Sumter, the Confederates occupied it, digging in for the next two years under heavy bombardment and preventing the Union from taking Charleston.

In June of 1863, Union troops gained control of Folly Island and the mouth of the Stono River. On July 10 they crossed Lighthouse Inlet to the southern end of Morris Island and by nightfall had secured half of the island and were within artillery range of Fort Sumter, which by then had become a symbol of Confederate resistance. Defending the tip of Morris Island and Charleston at the place formerly known as White Point Garden was the Confederate Battery Wagner.

On July 18 the Union forces advanced up the beach. It was this battle that was depicted in the film *Glory,* starring Morgan Freeman, Matthew Broderick, and Denzel Washington. Spearheading the attack was the Fifty-fourth Massachusetts Regiment under the leadership of Colonel Robert G. Shaw, the 25-year-old son of a wealthy Boston abolitionist. The bloody battle saw more than 40 percent of the black troops killed; Colonel Shaw died with them.

The courage of the Fifty-fourth proved once and for all to the leaders of the North and the South that black soldiers could fight. By 1865 a total of 178,895 black soldiers had enlisted in the Union Army—more than 12 percent of the North's fighting force. Recent Southern historical work has shown that black soldiers also fought with the Confederacy.

By September the Union controlled all of Morris Island, only 1,300 yards of water away from Fort Sumter. For almost two more years, the Confederates held out under more heavy bombardment. Finally in February of 1865 they withdrew in the night when they knew Charleston city was falling to Sherman.

Today The Battery, filled with war memorials, cannons, and a monument on the spot where the pirate Stede Bonnet was hanged, is one of the most pleasant parks in the city and is the ideal place for turning the kids loose.

You might follow the custom of hundreds of old Charlestonians who believe that no evening is complete without watching the sun set from here and then lighting up a cigar and taking a luxurious stroll along the ancient seawall.

Moving up the Charleston peninsula, across from the visitor center, is **The Charleston Museum** at 360 Meeting St. This is the first and oldest museum in the country, founded in 1773. Some exhibits focus on the Native Americans who were here first, others on the Revolutionary War or the Civil War; another celebrates the birth of the Charleston dance. Children will especially enjoy the Kidstory exhibit with amazing interactive displays. Toys, games, clothes, and even children's furniture have been collected from the past for entertainment and education. For a full grasp of old Charleston's culture and contributions to the country and to the world, no trip would be complete without a visit here. Adult tickets are $10 and children's are $5. Call (843) 722-2996 or visit charlestonmuseum.org.

Charleston has long prided itself on religious tolerance, evidenced by the fact that here you can find the oldest Baptist, Catholic, and Jewish houses of worship in the country.

The oldest of these is the **First Baptist Church** at 61 Church St. Founded in 1682, the church was redesigned in 1820 by Robert Mills, the first American-born architect and the designer of the Washington Monument. This structure is one of the earliest Greek Revival buildings in the nation. Morning services and Sunday school are held here on Sunday. Wednesday is Family Night, with supper and a prayer service. A concert series here features organ recitals and chamber music programs. Call (843) 722-3896 or see fbcharleston.org.

In 1839 **St. Mary's Church** was built at 89 Hasell St. This is the oldest Roman Catholic church congregation (founded in 1789) in the Carolinas and Georgia. The church is famous for its stained-glass windows, oil paintings, and graveyard. Call (843) 722-7696 or visit catholic-doc.org/saintmarys.

Kahal Kadosh Beth Elohim, at 90 Hasell St., was founded in 1749 and is the oldest synagogue in continuous use in the United States. According to synagogue records, it is the oldest surviving Reform synagogue in the world. Services are held Friday evenings and Saturday mornings. Call (843) 723-1090 or go to kkbe.org.

St. Michael's Episcopal Church, on the corner of Meeting and Broad Streets near the Four Corners of Law at 71 Broad St., was established in 1761.

The simple and elegant structure with a walled graveyard has long been a landmark and can be seen in many of the paintings and photographs of the old city. Call (843) 723-0603 or see stmichaelschurch.net. Another beautiful

South Carolina's Jewish Tradition

Jews have lived in South Carolina for more than 300 years. The provisions for religious tolerance offered by Carolina's Fundamental Constitution were unique for the time, and news of the friendly environment spread across Europe and the West Indies. Most of Carolina's early Jews were people of Sephardic heritage whose ancestors had been expelled from Spain and Portugal centuries earlier.

Over 100 years before the Civil War, hundreds of Jewish immigrants came to South Carolina from Prussia and Poland. They were attracted to the Charleston area by the busy port, by the already established Jewish community and synagogues, and by the opening of the back country to settlers. Early settlers opened dry-goods stores and became doctors, lawyers, journalists, and soldiers. Later they would fan out across North Carolina and into Georgia until every market town was served by at least one Jewish-owned shop. As time passed, they ran the stores that were the very center of the community. They served the farmers who would come into town, buy things they needed, and run up accounts, which would be paid when crops came in.

In Charleston between 1905 and 1912, the Jewish population more than doubled. The neighborhood where they settled was called Little Jerusalem. At one time some 40 stores on upper King Street were closed on Saturday, the Jewish Sabbath. The men held daily prayer services; the women kept kosher homes. They trained their African-American help to make potato kugel and gefilte fish, and they in turn were taught to fix fried chicken, corn bread, and okra gumbo.

Here is part of Isaac Harby's letter to Secretary of State James Monroe in 1816: "Jews are by no means to be considered as a religious sect, tolerated by the government: they constitute a portion of the People . . . Quakers and Catholics; Episcopalians and Presbyterians, Baptists and Jews, all constitute one great political family."

Rabbi Gustavus Pozanski, consecrating Kahal Kadosh Beth Elohim's new building in Charleston in 1841, said, "This synagogue is our temple, this city our Jerusalem, this happy land our Palestine."

And the last lines of Myer Moses' service before the Charleston Hebrew Orphan Society on October 15, 1906, may very well say it all: "Collect together thy long scattered people, and let their gathering place be in this land of milk and honey."

church is **St. Philip's Episcopal,** 146 Church St., in the "bend of Church Street" near the corner of Church and Queen Streets. Both of these churches have been lovingly sketched and painted by Elizabeth O'Neill Verner; prints of these sketches are modestly priced and are available at the Gibbes Museum of Art gift shop, 135 Meeting St.

Emanuel African Methodist Episcopal Church, 110 Calhoun St., was organized in 1787. Its present building has been in use since 1891. With its congregation of more than 1,600 members, the church is very active in assisting the Charleston Interfaith Crisis Ministry as well as a score of charitable organizations. Two Sunday morning worship services are held here. A Thursday evening service and a Bible study group on Wednesday are also offered. Call (843) 722-2561 or see emanuelame church.org.

Gardens & Historic Plantations

Not only is there a lot to see and do in Charleston, but there is also a great deal just outside the city limits on the barrier islands—namely, Isle of Palms, Sullivan's Island, Wadmalaw, Seabrook, and Kiawah. South of Charleston on Highway 17, the Savannah Highway, you'll see the sign for Seabrook and Kiawah Islands. Turn here on Main Road to Bohicket Road and proceed exactly 7.3 miles to the sign for **Angel Oak** and turn right. The sandy road will look deserted (because it is), and you'll think you're on the wrong road. But stay with it for about a half mile and you'll see a sight you will never, ever forget—the Angel Oak. It's one of the true American wonders. Don't forget your camera for this one. Best of all, admission is free. Call (843) 559-3496 for more information.

The Angel Oak may be the oldest living thing east of the Mississippi River—estimated at more than 1,400 years old. A few Angel Oak specifics: height 65 feet; circumference 25.5 feet; area of shade 17,000 square feet; largest limb circumference 11.25 feet; largest limb length 89 feet. In other words, it has to be seen to be believed.

Backtrack just a bit to the intersection of Bohicket and Maybank High-way (Highway 700) and head toward Wadmalaw Island. Continue until you see the signs on the left for the **Charleston Tea Plantation** at 6617 May-bank. No, they won't read your tea leaves here, but they will show you all about how tea is grown, harvested, and produced to make American Classic Tea. You can take a factory tour and a trolley tour through the scenic 127-acre farm, America's only tea garden. You can even bring your own picnic and spend the afternoon. Of course, you'll have to take home a couple of your favorite flavors and maybe a teapot or two for your daughter or your neighbor collecting the mail while you're gone. Call (843) 559-0383, ext. 206, to schedule a visit, or take a look at charlestonteaplantation.com.

In the opposite direction, 14 miles northwest of Charleston on Highway 61, is the site of America's oldest landscaped garden, at **Middleton Place,** 4300 Ashley River Rd. The plantation was laid out on the banks of the Ashley River, and the grounds include a fascinating museum house in a restored flanker to the original mansion, a modern inn, and one of the world's most beautiful gardens.

A recent addition to the exhibits at Middleton is an actual freedman's dwelling, furnished as it was in the 1870s when it was lived in by freed slaves who stayed on the plantation after the emancipation. You will also see blacksmiths, potters, weavers, and carpenters who will explain and demonstrate what they are doing and tell you about the plantation's history. The main house was built prior to 1741 but was burned by Union troops in 1865. As the story goes, the soldiers drank wine and had a glorious dinner with heavy silver and fancy linen at the main house, then they set fire to it and left.

Perhaps the best part of Middleton Place is the incredible view from the high terraces of the azalea, camellia, and rose gardens that roll down the hill into the Butterfly Lakes. The restaurant here serves authentic Low Country dishes for lunch, and they prepare a wonderful candlelight dinner. The gift shop sells plantation-crafted wares, books, and fine gifts for discerning guests. During the Spoleto Festival, Middleton often serves as the site for the grand finale. With the Spoleto Orchestra playing on a stage built over the Butterfly Lakes against a backdrop of fireworks, the huge crowd sits on blankets under the stars. What a concert! Open daily from 9 a.m. to 5 p.m. Call (843) 556-6020 or (800) 782-3608, or visit middletonplace.org.

Continuing on Highway 61, turn right at Highway 165 and in a few miles you'll come to **Summerville,** one of the most charming towns in the South. Formerly a winter resort for Charlestonians and Columbians, its streets ramble in curves through the trees. The lavish blooms of azaleas, camellias, and wisteria glow against the dark background of pines. Small boys still rush out to your car if they suspect you're a tourist, holding up signs marked GUIDE. Only two blocks from the business section is the *Azalea Park and Bird Sanctuary.* More than 800 specimens of native plants grow in the park. In the winter thousands of migratory birds stop here on their way south.

Summerville is a delightful town, and you will see not only enormous areas covered with azaleas and camellias but also hedges and ornamental shrubs of tea plants. Back in 1890 Dr. Charles U. Shepard began experimentation in commercial tea growing, and for a short time Lipton Tea helped finance his enterprise. His farm eventually failed, but the growing of tea for commercial purposes has resurfaced again on nearby Wadmalaw Island at the Charleston Tea Plantation. The knowledge of planting tea lived on in Summerville and can be seen all over town in the hedges and ornamental shrubs. Incidentally, the tea plant is a close cousin of the camellia.

Heading back toward Charleston on Highway 61, about 5 miles after passing Middleton Place again, you will see *Magnolia Plantation and Gardens,* at 3550 Ashley River Rd. The 300-year-old plantation is the ancestral home of South Carolina's illustrious Drayton family; 10 generations have used it since 1676. Internationally famous, it is considered to be one of America's oldest man-made attractions. Noted for its springtime beauty, it features more than 250 varieties of azalea and 900 varieties of camellia, as well as beautiful seasonal blooms every month of the year.

This is an ideal place for the kids. You can paddle a canoe through the waterways of the 125-acre waterfowl refuge, a former rice field, or view it from a wildlife observation tower along its walkways. Children will also enjoy Magnolia's petting zoo, where they can feed and pet a score of animals. Even your own pets are welcome here—as long as they stay on a leash. An interesting addition at Magnolia in the wildlife preserve is The Audubon Swamp Garden, which is 60 acres of black water in a cypress and tupelo swamp. The garden is accessible via boardwalks and dikes and is home to every species of Low Country wildlife. To reach Magnolia Gardens from Charleston, drive 10 miles west on Highway 61. You'll see the signs. Magnolia Gardens is open 8 a.m. to 5:30 p.m. every day (9 a.m. to 4:30 p.m. Nov through Feb). Admission is $15 for adults and teenagers, $10 for children ages 6 to 12, and free for children under age 6, with additional fees for the historic house and other attractions. Call (843) 571-1266 or (800) 367-3517, or visit magnoliaplantation.com.

If you're still in a visiting-a-garden mood after you've visited Magnolia Plantation and Gardens, you're only 12 miles from **Cypress Gardens,** a 162-acre swamp garden created in the 1920s and festooned with flower-lined pathways. Each spring a profusion of azaleas, dogwoods, daffodils, and wisteria is reflected in the mirrors of the black waters. Outdoor enthusiasts and bird-watchers will particularly enjoy the two rambling nature trails here, which wind through habitats and nesting areas for the alligator, pileated woodpecker, river otter, barred owl, and wood duck. You can explore the gardens in the traditional manner, with a guided flat-bottomed boat tour, or you can rent a canoe and paddle yourself off the beaten trail to who knows where.

From Charleston take I-26 to exit 208 (Moncks Corner). Follow Highway 52 north a couple of miles and watch for signs to Cypress Gardens. It is open daily from 9 a.m. to 5 p.m. Admission for adults is $10, seniors pay $9, children 6 through 12 pay $5, and children under 6 are admitted free. Call (843) 553-0515 or visit cypressgardens.org.

In the general area of Magnolia Plantation and Gardens and Middleton Place along Highway 171, between I-26 and Highway 17, is **Charles Towne Landing State Historic Site.** This is where you'll find the first permanent English settlement in the state and the birthplace of South Carolina. Today this newly refurbished and freshly interpreted park is preserved as a national treasure—a one-of-a-kind state park filled with history and natural splendor. The Landing is also a great place for children. Here they can see the *Adventure,* a full-scale replica of a 17th-century trading vessel at its wharf landing site. They can explore 80 acres of lush gardens or walk through the winding trails of the natural-habitat zoo, which features wolves, pumas, bears, and bison. A hands-on activities exhibit for the kids uses household tools and crafts common in the 17th century. Admission is $7.50 for adults and $3.50 for children ages 6 to 15. The park is open daily from 9 a.m. to 5 p.m. For further information contact Charles Towne Landing, 1500 Old Town Rd., Charleston 29407; call (843) 852-4200; or check out southcarolina parks.com/ctl.

And finally, one more plantation! **Boone Hall** is the one everyone wants to see—the plantation that was featured in the TV miniseries *North* *and South*. The entrance alone, through two magnificent columns of 88 live oaks, is worth the price of admission. Captain Thomas Boone planted 100 live oaks in 1743, and, amazingly enough, 88 have survived. Visitors can tour the (ca. 1930s) Greek Revival–style mansion and walk through the azalea and camellia gardens. Nine original slave cabins from the 18th century are also here. Boone Hall is 8 miles north of Charleston on Highway 17 at 1235 Long Point Rd., Mount Pleasant. Admission is $19.50 for adults, $17 for senior citizens and military, and $9.50 for children ages 6 through 12. Children under 6 are admitted free. Open all year, unless closed for one of their many special events. Apr through Labor Day, hours are 8:30 a.m. to 6:30 p.m. daily except Sun, when hours are noon to 5 p.m. Open the rest of the year from 9 a.m. to 5 p.m. daily except Sun, when hours are noon to 5 p.m. Call (843) 884-4371 or see boonehall plantation.com.

Other "Off the Peninsula" Stops

If you see a hawk, eagle, owl, vulture, falcon, kite, or osprey—any raptor—on the side of the road that has been hit by a car and is in trouble, *there is something you can do about it*. Wrap the bird up in a towel and place it in a dark box or trunk if it's not too hot. You must keep it out of the light. Then call the **South Carolina Center for Birds of Prey** at (843) 971-7474. Or, you may go to thecenterforbirdsofprey.org for more information. They will arrange for you to drop the injured bird off at a convenient place where their staff, or one of their countless volunteers, will pick it up and take it to their

Facts about Raptors

- A red-tailed hawk, if it could read, could read the *New York Times* from a mile away. It can also kill a full-size crow by merely squeezing it with its talons.

- An owl can swivel its head 270 degrees.

- An osprey, if it finds that you can see into its nest, will build it higher.

- An osprey carries fish with the head forward and the tail behind to limit drag.

headquarters on Highway 17 north of Charleston. As a matter of fact, if you are in some state other than South Carolina, you can still call that number or visit that website and they will give you the number of the nearest Birds of Prey Recovery Hospital.

The center, founded by Jim Singleton of Charleston, is a modern, well-equipped hospital owned and supported by tax-free contributions only and is probably one of the finest and best-managed in the entire Southeast. When they receive an injured bird, they quickly X-ray it to find out the damage, then they set the bones, treat it, and place it in a holding area where in most cases it recovers. Every year they treat and release more than 200 raptors.

A couple of years ago, they reset a bald eagle's wing and kept him in their holding building for weeks to make sure the wing had healed properly. I was there when they released it, and I'm here to say it was a sight to see. First of all, the bird had a wingspan of 5 to 6 feet, and when it took off, you could see the pine straw and the leaves on the ground move and you could feel the breeze. He flew to a pine tree limb about 100 yards away, took a long look around to get his bearings, said his good-byes, and headed out for Colorado—where he was probably from. For smaller birds that are injured, I guess the best bet is the Audubon Society. Oh, and what happens to birds that recover and still can't fly away? These birds are given a happy home right here and are used in educational projects throughout the state.

Staying in the East Cooper area, you'll find the popular ***Shem Creek Bar and Grill*** at 508 Mill St., Mount Pleasant, where they pride themselves on "cookin' on the Creek." This is the home of Sloppy John's Oyster Bar and Dock. Shem's is also accessible by water, and boats park right at the bar. They specialize in grilled seafood and beef, served indoors or outdoors on the "gazebos" overlooking Shem Creek. The place is big and at times noisy, but it has a wonderful, salty ambience, fine food, and an excellent staff. The kids will like the mounted river otter on display right across from the cashier. Lunches range from $6 to $15; dinners from $12 to $25. Open year-round. Call (843) 884-8102 or check out shemcreekbar andgrill.com.

On the harbor side of Shem Creek you'll find ***Vickery's,*** at 1313 Shrimp Boat Ln. They serve Cuban food and Low Country cuisine, as well as excellent seafood. This is a big and busy place and has nice outdoor seating overlooking the creek. Open daily, 11:30 a.m. to 1 a.m. Price range here is $9 to $19. Wine is available. Call (843) 884-4440 or go to vickerys.com.

Patriot's Point Naval and Maritime Museum is in Charleston Harbor and is one of the most unusual and best-run museums in the country. A mile from the dramatic Arthur Ravenel Jr. Bridge over the Cooper River are 2 permanently moored ships, 20 aircraft, and the World War II aircraft carrier *Yorktown*. You will find the destroyer *Laffey* and the submarine *Clamagore*, which can be boarded, inspected, and photographed at your leisure. Again, be sure to pack your digital camera and snap away.

To give you some idea of the size and weight of the *Yorktown,* consider this: During Hurricane Hugo in 1989, which practically lifted Charleston up and set it back down again, the carrier barely moved. The ship served in combat at Truk, the Marianas, Iwo Jima, and Okinawa in World War II. Later it picked up the crew of *Apollo VIII,* the first manned spacecraft to circle the moon.

The hangar and flight decks of the carrier are now set up as a journey through the history of naval aviation. Here you'll see many of the prop-driven fighters, bombers, and torpedo planes that fought throughout the Pacific. You'll see a B-25 bomber similar to the ones of General Jimmy Doolittle's famous "Sixty Seconds Over Tokyo" raid in addition to fighters that provided the air support during the Korean War. A great collection of some of the world's most feared jets is displayed here, along with distinguished battle histories spanning from Korea to Desert Storm. You'll see the actual living quarters of the pilots and the "ready rooms" where they were briefed on their upcoming missions.

Hurricane Hugo

After Hugo whipped through Charleston in 1989, it left a number of stories behind that seem to increase and get bigger every year. One is of the farmer who tied six chickens to six posts, hoping they wouldn't get blown away. The idea worked, and the chickens all lived to see another day—unfortunately the storm suction pulled out every single feather of every single bird. And the best line that's still around came from a mobile-home owner: "Man, when I looked outside in the morning there were refrigerators in the trees."

While aboard the carrier, you'll also want to stop by the ship's theater for a complimentary viewing of the 1944 Academy Award–winning film *The Fighting Lady,* which features some of the most incredible World War II dog-fight footage ever taken. The centerpieces on board the *Yorktown* are the 20 vintage aircraft ranging from a World War II basic trainer to the jets that ruled the skies of the Korean, Vietnam, and Persian Gulf Wars. They even have a World War II torpedo bomber much like the one former president George Herbert Walker Bush pancaked in the Pacific.

The museum is open daily from 9 a.m. to 6:30 p.m. Admission is $18 for adults, $15 for seniors and active-duty military with ID (active duty in uniform are free), $11 for children ages 6 through 11, and free for children under 6. Parking is $5. Call (843) 884-2727 or visit patriotspoint.org.

If you're staying overnight in Charleston, the **Spiritline Dinner Cruise** is one of the musts on your list. Get on board the *Spirit of Carolina,* which leaves from Patriots Point in Mount Pleasant, for a three-hour evening of dinner, live entertainment, and the best possible view of the old city at dark. It's a beautiful trip and one you won't soon forget. The food, entertainment, and service are excellent. It gets cool out in the harbor, so take along a sweater.

Spiritline also offers a one-and-a-half-hour sightseeing trip in the daytime and a two-and-a-quarter-hour trip out to the Fort Sumter National Monument and Museum. These two tours depart from both Patriots Point and downtown Charleston. Call (843) 722-2628 or (800) 789-3678 for information, or go to spiritlinecruises.com. The price for the dinner cruise Sun through Thurs is about $50 per person. On Fri and Sat, it's in the $55 range. Prices for the Harbor Tour are $17 per person, $10 for children ages 6 to 11, and free for children under 6. Prices for the Fort Sumter Tour are adults $17, children ages 6 to 11 $10, and children under 6 free.

Momma Brown's at 2840 Highway 17, Mount Pleasant, is hard, hard, hard to beat. In the Carolina sweepstakes on barbecue, they're way out in front of the pack; no one else is even close. They specialize in the great vinegar-and-pepper-based sauce that is famous down here in the Low Country. Open Mon through Sat from 11 a.m. to 9 p.m. and Sun 11 a.m. to 3 p.m.; closed Mon. Prices vary from $5 to $10. Call (843) 849-8802.

At 778 S. Shelmore Blvd. (in the Bi-Lo Shopping Center), Mount Pleasant, **Langdon's Restaurant and Wine Bar** specializes in Low Country cuisine with an updated and sophisticated twist. Prices range from around

$15 to $50 for dinner. Open Mon through Sat from 11:30 a.m. to 2 p.m. for lunch and at 5 p.m. for dinner. Call (843) 388-9200 or go to langdons restaurant.com.

Atlanticville Restaurant and Cafe, at 2063 Middle St., Sullivan's Island, is located in a traditional island beach house, where you can sit on the patio before or after dinner and watch the sunset. Inside, the atmosphere is casual but the food is elegant, and there is an extensive wine list. One of the features here is Thai Tuesday, which is very popular with the natives. Open daily from 5:30 to 10 p.m.; Sunday brunch from 10 a.m. to 2 p.m. Prices range from $25 to $35 for dinner. Call (843) 883-9452. Their website is atlanticville.net.

Crossing back through the Holy City and over the Ashley River in the South Windemere Shopping Center, is the Mediterranean Bistro, or *Med Bistro,* at 90 Folly Rd. Their specialties are pasta, seafood, sandwiches, and dinners, priced from $8 to $24, along with a huge wholesale arrangement for buying wine. The Med is open from 11 a.m. to 10 p.m. Mon through Sat and serves lunch ($7 to $10) until 2 p.m. Sunday brunch is from 9:30 a.m. to 3:30 p.m. Call (843) 766-0323 or visit themedbistro.com.

Another amazing place, especially for eating South Carolina seafood, is *Bowen's Island* at 1870 Bowen's Island Rd. This unique restaurant is as rustic and back-roads as it can get. As a matter of fact, unless you're ready for it, you'll take one look, hit reverse, and back right on out. But stick with it. First off, you have to find it. The best bet is to stop in the Folly Beach area and ask anyone. Everyone goes here and has been going here forever. Once you get over the shock of seeing it, you'll love it. Everything is fresh because for years the Bowens have been running the whole show—from procuring the seafood to cleaning it to getting it on the table. The dress code is ultra-casual, which means jeans are the top of the line.

A fire gutted the old concrete-block restaurant, where the walls were covered with names and one-liners that went back to the 1940s. A new elevated open-air building has taken its place and is gradually taking on its own personality as patrons pen new graffiti while enjoying the creekside breezes and sunset views. Get here early and tour the holding tanks for the crabs and find out why Folly Beach oysters are the best on the coast. If you have any questions about crabs, oysters, clams, and seafood in general (such as how to tell when it's fresh or questionable or really off-limits), this is the place to find out the answers. The specialties here are fried shrimp, crab cakes, and all-you-can-eat oysters at prices you can't beat. Once again, don't be put off by the outside appearance; inside, once the food is served and the ancient jukebox is on, it's terrific. Open Tues through Sat from 5 to 10 p.m. Prices range from $10 to $15 tops. Call (843) 795-2757 or take a look at bowensislandrestaurant.com.

A few years back I wrote a book titled *Golfing in the Carolinas*. The assignment was simply to pick out the 50 courses in the Carolinas that I liked best, play each of them, write a few words, and then go on to the next one. I learned a great deal on my tour, especially about master architects Donald Ross, Alister McKenzie, Robert Trent Jones, Tom Fazio, and Pete Dye, whom I watched build the **Ocean Course** on Kiawah Island. This course, which hosted the 1991 Ryder Cup matches and the 2012 PGA Championship, is an absolute must for any golfer with a set of sticks. Incidentally, you go right by the Angel Oak on your way here (see "Gardens and Historic Plantations," earlier in this chapter).

Ten of the Ocean Course holes run right along the ocean. Considering the cost of oceanfront lots on Kiawah, the course may very well be one of the most expensive ever built. It is certainly the hardest to play. When the wind is up, which is almost every afternoon, very few golfers break 90. During the '91 Ryder Cup matches, pros were actually aiming into the gallery hoping to avoid the howling wind, and the pro Mark Calcavecchia was reduced to actual tears—he had to withdraw from the final holes. While windblown and terrifying, the Ocean Course is a course all golfers should play just to be able to say they tried it. Fortunately it's semiprivate, and a simple phone call to (843) 768-2121 or (800) 654-2924 can get you a tee time. Try to come early to avoid the afternoon wind, and bring plenty of balls. See kiawahisland.com.

golfcourses

While Charleston and the Low Country are only 5 to 10 feet above sea level, the land rises to 3,533 feet 200 miles away at Sassafras Mountain, west of Greenville. This elevation difference, along with the great varieties of trees and soil, accounts for the fact that South Carolina is considered by many to be the best state in the country for its variety of great golf courses.

While South Carolina doesn't have such venerable courses as Shinnecock out on Long Island, New York, or Brookline near Boston, it has something else—incredible golf weather. When you consider that northern courses are closed down four and five months a year and that down here in the so-called hard lard belt we play almost every day, the rest of the golfing country simply pales by comparison. South Carolina also has a wonderful variety of courses, ranging from the 4,000-foot mountain courses to the sandhills to the Low Country and the ocean. While most northern courses are private, most of South Carolina's are semiprivate, which means a great number of golfers will have the opportunity to play on a wide variety of great courses. A few of the better ones include Tom Fazio's famous ***Harbor Course at Wild Dunes*** on The Isle of Palms (843) 886-2164, (800) 845-8880, ext. 2, or wilddunes.com; ***Arthur Hill's Dunes West*** in Mount Pleasant, (843) 856-9000 or golfduneswest.com; and Pete Dye's aforementioned Ocean Course on Kiawah. For more on all of Kiawah's golf courses, see kiawahresort.com.

Because Charleston offers so much to the visiting tourist, it may very well be the ideal city for the "golf widow" and the ever-growing number of "golf widowers." Cases are on file of golfers who arrive here determined to play four or five of the dozen famous courses around town but who, after looking at the calendar of events, the long list of great restaurants, and the sights to be seen, wind up not getting a single club out of their bags. But for the golfer who has to play, this is the place to do it. The truly spectacular courses here, which year in and year out make the list of the top 50 in the country, are the Ocean Course on Kiawah Island and at Wild Dunes on Isle of Palms.

For the golf historian, a trip out to the private ***Charleston Country Club*** on James Island should be fascinating. Despite the records showing that the first course in America was open for play in 1898 at St. Andrews in Yonkers, New York, the game was being played here almost 250 years earlier under the encouragement of King Charles II. King Charles was an avid golfer, and a 1698 print shows him being interrupted in the middle of a round to read news of an Irish rebellion. At the club you can see the old menus from the late 17th century and golf notices from the early 18th century. For information call the club at (843) 795-0422 or visit countryclub ofcharleston.com.

Places to Stay in Charleston & the Surrounding Area

CHARLESTON

Ashley Inn Bed & Breakfast
201 Ashley Ave.
(843) 723-1848, (800) 581-6658
charleston-sc-inns.com

Charleston Marriott Hotel
170 Lockwood Dr.
(843) 723-3000, (866) 357-6667
visitusahotels.com

Francis Marion Hotel
387 King St.
(843) 722-0600, (877) 756-2121
francismarioncharleston.com

John Rutledge House Inn
116 Broad St.
(843) 723-7999, (800) 476-9741
charminginns.com

Middleton Inn
4290 Ashley River Rd.
(843) 556-0500, (800) 543-4774
theinnatmiddletonplace.com

Wentworth Mansion
149 Wentworth St.
(843) 853-1886, (888) 466-1886
charminginns.com

MONCK'S CORNER

Rice Hope Plantation Inn
206 Rice Hope Dr.
(843) 849-9000
ricehope.com

Places to Eat in Charleston & the Surrounding Area

CHARLESTON

Anson
12 Anson St.
(843) 577-0551
ansonrestaurant.com

Coast
39-D John St.
(843) 722-8838
coastbarandgrill.com

Marina Variety Store and Restaurant
City Marina,
17 Lockwood Dr.
(843) 723-6325
varietystorerestaurant.com

Peninsula Grill
Planters Inn,
112 N. Market St.
(843) 723-0700
peninsulagrill.com

Tommy Condon's Irish Pub & Seafood Restaurant
160 Church St.
(843) 577-3818
tommycondons.com

WEST ASHLEY

Mustard Seed
1970 Maybank Hwy.
(843) 762-0072
dinewithsal.com

MT. PLEASANT

R.B.'s Seafood Restaurant and Raw Bar
97 Church St.
(843) 881-0466
rbsonshemcreek.com

THE SOUTHERN CORNER

Barrier Islands

Prepare to have your breath taken away by the scenery here. South of Charleston and all the way to Savannah, Georgia, 100 miles away, the land stays only a few feet above sea level and has a border of sandy barrier islands. Tall cypress trees rise above the live oaks and longleaf pines, and the rivers feeding into the inlets and the ocean are a dark tea color, owing to the tannic acid from the cypress and swamp roots. In the narrow strip of lowland along the coast is the subtropical growth in which are found such plants as the large palmetto, several dwarf palmettos, yucca, and evergreen holly. The grasses along the coast are panicum, water millet, and sea oats, all of which are necessary to sustain the life of the rolling dunes protecting the shoreline from wind and tidal erosion. The people along Highway 17, working small truck farms and commuting to Charleston and Hilton Head for work, have changed very little in the last hundred years.

As you travel on Highway 17, especially on the long section south of Charleston, you'll be traveling through a

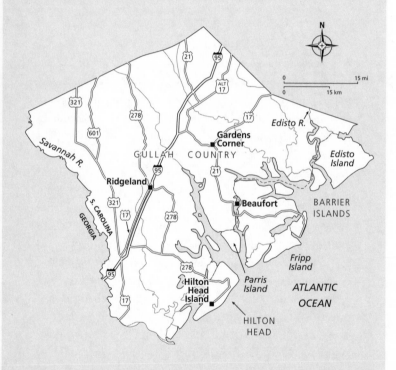

part of the South that has withstood much of the tides of change. For a deeper insight and appreciation you might read *Praying for Sheetrock* by Melissa Fay Greens. In a wonderful storytelling style, she tells of the old road and marvelously captures much of the African-American culture.

Before you begin a tour of the **Edisto Island** area, which is this chapter's first destination, here's a little history. In 1666 Robert Sandford's British expedition dropped anchor at Edisto Island and spent a pleasant week with the Edistow Indians. They were helpful, cordial, and friendly, and the delighted Sandford went back to London and spread the news that this was the ideal place for a British colony. While he was gone, the Edistows had second thoughts. When the settlers returned, the Edistows told them they had changed their minds about tourists settling among them and that the natives up in Kiawah country a few miles north were not only much friendlier but were actually looking for newcomers and would welcome them with open arms. The settlers got the message, weighed anchor, sailed back up the coast, and settled Charleston on the banks of the Ashley River.

TOP RECOMMENDATIONS IN THE SOUTHERN CORNER

African Village
Near Sheldon
(843) 846-8900
oyotunji.org

The Beaufort Bookstore
2127 Boundary St.
Beaufort
(843) 525-1066
beaufortbookssc.com

The Edisto Island Museum
8123 Chisholm Plantation Rd.
Edisto Island
(843) 869-1954
edistomuseum.org

Red Piano Too Art Gallery
870 Sea Island Pkwy.
St. Helena
(843) 838-2241
redpianotoo.com

Rhett House Inn
1009 Craven St.
Beaufort
(843) 524-9030
rhetthouseinn.com

Sheldon Church Ruins
Highway 21 and 235
Near Gardens Corner

In 1674 Edisto Island was purchased from the Indians by the Earl of Shaftsbury. Shortly after, Paul Grimball was granted 600 acres of land on the North Edisto River and built a plantation house. In 1686 Spanish marauders sacked the area and the plantation and destroyed the **Grimball Plantation.** Today, the remains of the foundation (made of tabby, which is a cement made of lime, sand or gravel, and crushed oyster shells) can still be seen near the river.

One hundred years before the British, the Spanish built a small mission here on the banks of St. Peire's Creek. Called Oristo, a variant on the Indian word *Edistow,* the mission was operated by members of the Jesuit Order. Today, only a single place name, Spanish Mount Point, recalls that period more than 300 years ago.

Not far from the ruins of the Grimball Plantation at **Point of Pines** is an old graveyard of the early settlers. Unfortunately, the slate gravestones have worn smooth over the years and are barely legible, but if you look closely, you can see some of the dates are before 1700.

The Edisto Island Historic Preservation Society runs **The Edisto Island Museum,** located at 8123 Chisolm Plantation Rd. Each room is crowded with displays, books, old letters, and artifacts that trace the history of the island from the time of the Edistow Indians. One of the many attractions is an electronically controlled nature board on which you match animal prints to the animals. Kids love this; adults are baffled and generally give up fast. The museum is open Tues through Sat from 1 to 4 p.m. Admission is $4 for adults, $2 for students, and free for children 10 and younger. Private tours can be arranged by calling (843) 869-1954. Their website is edistomuseum.org.

alligatornews

If the approximate distance from the eyes to the tip of the nose is 8 inches, that means the gator is 8 feet long. Ten inches means 10 feet, and so on. And one more tip: They actually love marshmallows. If you feel you have to feed them, do it from the bridges. And one last tip—DON'T.

Here on Edisto Island, you need to be aware that you share this rustic and historic real estate with more than a few alligators. If you see one, chances are there will be others nearby. **Note:** Keep kids and small dogs away from them. A fact no one seems to believe is that alligators have remarkable speed for 20 to 30 yards and have been known to do terrible damage to dogs, deer, children, and slow-witted adults.

Another hazard down here in the Low Country is snakes! Keep the children away from creek banks, drain ditches, heavy leaf-covered areas, and woods. South Carolina has the distinction of having the biggest variety of poisonous snakes in the country. As a matter of fact, Beaufort County, a few miles south of Edisto, is the place where most of the snakes used for extracting venom for snakebite serum are captured. They are also gathered for carnival shows as well as for a sprinkling of Pentecostal churches that still practice snake handling, or "snake chunking."

None of the snakes will attack unprovoked, but if you step on one or scare one, that is a different story. Some of the coral snakes are especially lethal. Beautiful and tiny with exquisite red and yellow bands, they look like toys, but as the locals say, "They can kill you quicker than a train." This is an exaggeration, but an untreated bite can be very dangerous. How do you tell a lethal coral snake from nonlethal? Simple rule:

> YELLOW ON BLACK, FRIENDLY JACK.
> BLACK ON YELLOW, WILL KILL A FELLOW.

Speaking of snakes, a definite qualifier for "off the beaten path" status is the ***Edisto Island Serpentarium*** at 1374 Highway 174. This is an indoor/outdoor museum facility dedicated exclusively to the recognition, preservation, and study of reptiles. Opened in 1999, the Serpentarium is the brainchild of two Edisto Island brothers, Ted and Heyward Clamp, and their more than 50 years of snake hunting in South Carolina and around the world. Here you'll find a wide variety of reptiles. Those not displayed indoors behind glass are viewed by visitors outdoors who look over low-walled enclosures to observe the snakes and other critters living in streams, climbing in trees, or basking on stumps or logs exactly as they would be seen if encountered in the wild. The hands-on staff is prepared to answer questions and demystify the understandable reluctance some may have for the subject matter. Admission is $13.95 for adults (13 and up), $9.95 for youngsters 4 to 12, and free for children younger than 4. Check out their website at edistoserpentarium.com.

Edisto, they say, is not so much a place as it is a time—and a time, preservationists add, that has resisted change. The old plantation money was made from indigo and sea-island cotton. Since enormous labor was needed for planting, tending, and harvesting these crops, the island became a major entry point for slaves from Africa and Barbados. The landowners sought out and secured the most educated slaves, and because many came from African aristocracy, race relations here were much different than they were in the rest of the state. Incidentally, the single-room-wide house construction so typically found in Charleston is said to come directly from Barbados.

One of the oldest stories here is of the very young white girl Hepzibah Jenkins, who was raised by local slaves when her mother died and her father was imprisoned during the Revolution. Later she married the island's largest landowner. Years passed, and in 1810 Hepzibah decided she wanted to build the plantation slaves a Baptist church. This inflamed her husband and the result was their separation. But Hepzibah was undaunted and started baking bread in a tabby oven (constructed of sea shells, lime, and sand) at what became the Hepzibah Jenkins Bakery. She financed and built the first church in America founded by a woman. The old bakery eventually disintegrated and became overgrown with vegetation, but the church, which is still called the Baptist Church, can be seen on the left side of Highway 174 as you enter Edisto. At the back of the church is the *grave of Hepzibah Jenkins,* and over it her children have erected a monument that reads:

> HER CHARACTER WAS SO STRONGLY CAST, AND HER IMPULSES WERE SO GENEROUS, THAT SHE WAS AN OBJECT OF INDIFFERENCE TO NO ONE. THE POOR AND THE AFFLICTED WERE SPECIAL OBJECTS OF HER CONSIDERATION. BY THEM HER LOSS IS TRULY FELT, AND BY US WHO KNEW HER BEST, SHE IS MOST LAMENTED.

Another incident that illustrates the tenacity and independence of the Edisto people occurred in 1861. It was then, when South Carolina was debating whether to sign the Ordinance of Secession, that the Edisto Island delegate jumped to his feet and declared that irrespective of what the state did, Edisto Island would secede from the Union all by itself.

In 1810 vacationers from Charleston and Columbia began coming to the Edisto beaches. That same year *Edingsville Island* was developed by one of the island's wealthy cotton planters, William Edings. By 1820 he had built 60 large summer cottages and a boardwalk; the resort was comparable to Atlantic City, New Jersey, or Newport, Rhode Island. Photographs of ladies with hoop skirts and parasols and men in skimmers can be seen in the Edisto Island Museum. Unfortunately, the hurricane of 1890 destroyed everything standing, and the island returned to its formerly barren state as the barrier island it had been. It wasn't until 1994 that the first new house was built here. These days, only a handful of homes are on the island. If splendid isolation (read: luxurious) sounds like your cup of tea, contact Vacation Rentals by Owner, listing #53342; visit vrbo.com/53342.

Highway 174 dead-ends at Palmetto Drive. At the corner is ***The Pavil-ion Restaurant,*** 102 Palmetto Blvd., open for dinner seven days a week and lunch Thurs through Mon. A good buy here (to share) is their steamed seafood pot, a medley of lobster tail, crab legs, oysters, clams, shrimp, corn, and sausage for $25. Beer and wine are served. Children are welcome and can be turned loose to walk along the beach. Call (843) 869-4474.

Dave Lybrand owns and helps operate ***Edisto Realty, Inc.,*** at 1405 Palmetto Blvd. Call (800) 856-6538 for reservations for beachfront houses and villas and also creekside rentals, or visit edistorealty.com. The variety of accommodations here is enormous. The Ocean Villa is rustic and right smack on the beach. The top floor has a huge porch overlooking the ocean where you can sunbathe, eat, drink, and be merry as you watch the long strings of pelicans gliding down the beach. I stayed here one year and counted 86 brown pelicans in one group; they often number more than 100. Private homes also are available for weekly rental. A beachfront house that sleeps eight averages $1,800 per week; houses off the beach range from about $600 to $1,200 in peak season.

Coming into Edisto, you'll spot the ***Old Post Office,*** 1442 Highway 174, the premier restaurant on the island. A couple of menu highlights include shrimp broiled with a mousseline sauce on whole-grain grits and a pecan-coated quail. A three-course dinner for two with wine should run you around $90. The chef, Cherry J. Smalls, is a native here and can whip up the best Southern fare in the Low Country. The Old Post Office serves dinner only, Tues through Sat. Reservations are required; dress is casual. Call (843) 869-2339 or check out theoldpostofficerestaurant.com.

Edisto Island, with more than 7 miles of uninterrupted beach, has managed to keep its landscape, skyline, and ecology about the way they were 20 or 30 years ago. It's still one of the real jewels on the South Carolina coastline. It's also one of the best areas in the entire country for collecting

Hurricane & Tornado Facts

A hurricane test: If you hold up a sheet of plywood to a window and turn it loose and it sticks, hammer it in and head for a shelter.

A test to see if you're in a hurricane: Check the rain—when it hits your window, it will flow up and not down. This is hard to believe until you see it. But if you do see it, it's too late.

During a hurricane, most fish and all shrimp go crazy and swim in circles, even leap in the air. Some of the smart ones, however, swallow rocks and sink to the bottom.

Birds fly low to the ground. Some get caught in the hurricane's eye and stay in it until the storm diminishes and thus wind up thousands of miles from home. Legend has it the snowy egret came from Africa in a hurricane eye.

During a hurricane dogs howl and run around in tight little dog circles. Horses get nervous and stamp the ground. Cats ignore it.

If you're in a mobile home, get out in a hurry.

If you're on the road, and you shouldn't be, don't stay in the car. Find the nearest concrete culvert and crawl, climb, or claw your way under and stay there.

If the eye comes over, keep in mind that the worst part may very well be on its way. This is especially true if you are in the 12-to-3 quadrant of the hurricane. Keep in mind the hurricane is spinning counterclockwise. This means the wind behind it—say it's

fossils. This is because this coastline was once a lengthy primordial bog, and today the tides and currents keep stirring it up. Sharks' teeth are easy to find, but they are nothing when compared to the fossils of some of the creatures that inhabited the area millions of years ago. Along these shores have been found the remains of elephants with tusks turned backwards, crocodiles 30 feet long, a 200-pound capybara (the biggest rodent in the world), birds with teeth and 19-foot wingspans, a ground sloth as big as a Volkswagen, horses with three toes, camels, tapirs, and saber-toothed tigers. Many vertebrate paleontologists still refer to the 1857 *Pliocene Fossils of South Carolina,* by Francis Holmes and Michael Tuomey, as the classic book about this science in the state.

Wyndam Ocean Ridge Resort is a 300-acre resort with one- and two-bedroom villas for rent by the night or the week. Call (877) 296-6335. Golf packages can be arranged for playing the **Plantation Course at Edisto**

at 30 miles an hour—pushes it 30 miles faster in the 12-to-3 quadrant and slows it down 30 miles in the 6-to-9. But don't take time to analyze this; get out of your car, stay out of mobile homes, and find that culvert.

The big killer in hurricanes down here is not the wind or the water but the locals who plug in home generators and forget to disconnect the outside line. What happens is someone will assume the line is dead and step on it or pick it up.

Another killer, almost as lethal, is chain saws. If you use one, make sure you don't under any conditions hold it above your head, and be absolutely certain your feet are planted firmly on something solid. You might also leave the beer in the car.

Tornadoes usually ride along on the edge of the hurricane and do tremendous damage. Since you won't be able to see them, there's no point in even watching for them. Just know they're out there and take every precaution.

For years churches were routinely destroyed during tornadoes, while the town saloons remained untouched. Finally a saloon keeper told a preacher to keep the church doors open the way he did. The preacher tried it and it worked. The word spread, and now churches and buildings of any kind leave their windows open when the storms threaten. So, wherever you're staying, crack your windows on each end when the storm warnings are announced.

Practical tip: Toss a few plastic gallon milk jugs (with tops) in your trunk. After a hurricane or a tornado they'll be worth their weight in gold for collecting and storing drinking water.

(843-869-1111). The course is right on the property; many of the villas overlook the fairways. As a matter of fact, you can step out on the fairway with a nine iron and a bag of balls and get in all the practice you need. The greens fees and cart rentals are the lowest in the entire area, which is a notable fact since this is a 6,400-yard absolutely first-class course with wonderful greens and enough tight fairways to give any golfer all the challenge he or she needs. As a matter of cold fact, water comes into play on 14 holes, and I'd suggest a long iron, rather than a wood, from many of the tees. The Tom Jackson–designed course was renovated in 2006, and the new four-bedroom Plantation Villas with en suite baths were added, providing a perfect accommodation for golfing groups.

Unlike most country clubs, where you have to know someone before you are allowed to pay—usually more than $100—to play, tee times here are unbelievably easy to arrange. All you have to do is show up at the pro shop with plenty of balls. In season greens fees are around $59, including a cart, and weekly rates are available. For the golfer whose spouse doesn't play, this is probably the best course in the state where you can take him/her out for a lesson and have a great time doing it. Between the greens and tees are some wonderful walks through the live oaks, palmettos, and magnolia trees. (**Caution:** When you walk near the lakes and creeks, keep your eyes peeled for the local alligators and an occasional snake. Armadillos, who have been spotted here recently, are harmless.) This is also a wonderful spot for bird-watching; you're sure to see three or four great blue herons and all the brown pelicans you can count. If your spouse doesn't play, take him/her with you anyway for the cart ride through this really wonderful and unique area. The course has an excellent restaurant between the 9th green and the 10th tee. One final suggestion: If you're planning on playing here, use the driving range at the other end of the island to warm up. For tee times or information, call (843) 869-1111 or visit theplantationcourseatedisto.com.

At the north end of the beach is ***Edisto Beach State Park.*** Though small, the campground is one of the prettiest in the state. Many of the sites are set on small hills under live oaks and look out on the ocean only a few yards away. The campground is equipped with electrical and water hookups, barbecue pits, and a place to shower. A grocery store is only a block away. For those who love to camp or for folks on a budget, this is the ideal place to stay. While here you can explore the nature trails or go fishing, crabbing, or sailing. It is also an excellent place for bird-watching. For further information write Edisto Beach State Park, 8377 State Cabin Rd., Edisto Island 29438; call (843) 869-2156; or visit southcarolinaparks.com.

For an elaborate rental house that is truly off the beaten path, call the Prudential Kapp/Lyons Agency at (843) 869-2516 or (800) 945-9667 and ask for information on ***Whitmarsh*** at the end of Botany Road. The road is canopied by a beautiful tunnel of live oaks shrouded with Spanish moss. Visit kapplyons.com.

Whitmarsh has six bedrooms and three and a half baths; it can sleep as many as 16. The price is around $2,095 per week in season, $1,395 off-season. The house, completely secluded and overlooking Frampton Inlet and the ocean, stands more than 40 feet high and, with its 180-degree view, has probably the best vista on the island. You can sit in the cocktail area at the top of the house and watch the leaping porpoises as they follow the shrimp boats into port in the afternoons. You will also see pelicans, egrets, herons, ospreys, ducks, geese, and even eagles. In the pastures off Botany Road, you can see egrets doing something rather strange. One egret will ride on a cow's back and pick off fleas, while two others high-step along in the grass eating the crickets and grasshoppers the cow flushes up. A little more bird lore here: Keep your eyes open—you may catch a glimpse of a Low Country painted bunting. This bird is a rare sight. With its blues, yellows, reds, and greens, it looks a great deal like a parrot straight out of the Amazon, only smaller.

You should also know that Edisto is a fishing paradise. You can fish here on the beach, from the creek banks, or from a john boat. John boats and surfing equipment can be rented for a nominal charge at **The Edisto Marina,** and you can fish almost anywhere you choose. They're at 3702 Dock Site Rd., (843) 869-3504. Many local residents simply cast their lines from the bridges into the creeks or the inlets. Fishing here, you'll meet some of the resident characters of the island, and you'll get enough fishing advice to last a lifetime. One line you might hear from someone speaking Gullah is "Most hook fish don' hep dry hominy," which means "The fish you almost caught doesn't do much for a plate of grits."

As you fish and watch the colors changing on the marsh grass and a long string of pelicans heading home right above you, you might consider what I. Jenkins Mikell, a plantation owner down here, once said: "Life here is one long dream. Here the art of being busy and doing nothing was brought to a fine point."

Leave Edisto on Highway 174, go to Highway 17, and turn left to Gardens Corner, roughly 15 miles away back on the mainland. The land here remains about the same—low and sandy with pine trees, magnolias, and a dozen varieties of oak. Turn left on Highway 21. Only 5 miles down the road is **Beaufort,** the second-oldest town in the state, settled in 1711. During the Civil War the town was occupied by Union forces, which saved it from being burned. Today the big homes looking out over the inlet and the ocean are almost exactly as they were in 1860. You can get a very good idea of the look of the old town and its surroundings from any one of the following movies filmed here: *Glory, The Big Chill, The Great Santini, Forrest Gump, Conrack,* and *The Prince of Tides.* As a matter of fact, Pat Conroy, author of *The Prince of Tides,* spent his childhood here and later taught school down the coast out on Daufuskie Island. And as another matter of fact, the cast of *The Prince of Tides*—Barbra Streisand, Nick Nolte, and Jeroen Krabbé—all stayed downtown at the Rhett House, one of the old mansions that have been converted to bed-and-breakfast inns. More on that later.

Your first stop should be the **Visitor Information Center** at 2001 Boundary St.; the phone number is (843) 986-5400 and their website is beaufortsc.org. Here you can pick up a walking-tour map with points of particular interest marked out. They will also help you with suggestions for restaurants and places to stay if you are spending the night, which you should do. Mornings here on Bay Street, with its very large and very beautifully landscaped park that runs along the waterfront, are wonderful. Stop in one of the restaurants or coffee shops that run along the park for a leisurely break with a serene view.

If you feel like walking a few miles, pick up a tour map and just follow the dotted lines. The map shows 34 historical sites, including **St. Helena's Episcopal Church** at 505 Church St., built in 1724, and the **Beaufort Museum,** located in the Arsenal (1798) at 713 Craven St., a fascinating repository of the city's man-made history. There's more at beaufort-sc.com. If you're not too keen on walking, a much easier way of seeing the old town is from the seat of one of the very comfortable horse-drawn carriages that are parked at the curb and available at almost any hour. Prices run around $20 and the tour lasts about 50 minutes. If you are so inclined, take the ride right around sundown with an iced bottle of white wine.

At 1009 Craven St. is the aforementioned and internationally famous **Rhett House Inn.** This bed-and-breakfast is the ideal place to stay in Beaufort, but you must make your reservations early. Actors, directors, and writers have been headquartering at this centerpiece long before *The Prince of Tides* was filmed in this area. The inn's hosts, Steve and Marianne Harrison, originally from New York, have a marvelous collection of candid photographs of Barbra Streisand, Nick Nolte, and Jeroen Krabbé all looking delighted with their accommodations and everything around them. Check the kitchen and ask the cook to show you the fascinating print that Krabbé gave the Harrisons.

This old mansion, which is as ornamental as a wedding cake, has wraparound verandas, classic columns and porticos, and beautifully carved and finished entries and staircases. Fresh flowers are everywhere, and each and every appointment is in excellent taste. Every room has a small library; the main library has everything from Vladimir Nabokov to Stephen King to Jackie Collins. All guest rooms have televisions, telephones, and private baths; two have fireplaces. You can even sleep in the same bed that Barbra Streisand slept in. The management will be glad to arrange golf, tennis, swimming, and massages. Carriage tours, sunset cruises, and historic walks are also available. Rates are $195 to $325. Call (843) 524-9030 or visit rhetthouseinn.com.

Steve and Marianne are delightful and knowledgeable company and love to talk far into the night about books, the theater, and the movies. The excellent gourmet dinners here feature regional favorites such as crab cakes, fresh fish, roast lamb, and vegetables with herbs from the Rhett House gardens. You can even dine on the porch under the limbs of the great live oak in the front yard. Room rates include not only wonderful accommodations but afternoon teas, bicycles, and a full breakfast. Smoking is limited to the porches, verandas, and garden. Ask about their seasonal "specials."

Two blocks from the Rhett House at 906 Port Republic St. is a little gem of a restaurant called **Emily's.** Featuring a unique menu that includes 29 different dishes called tapas, this is a spot that should not be overlooked. Just a few of the exotic dishes that represent the international flavor of the place are escargot Bourguignon, wild boar sausage, crabmeat Rangoon, and tempura shrimp. Emily's also has an excellent wine list. The bar at the end of the room is perfect for meeting a few of the more interesting local residents. Dress is casual. Open daily from 4 to 11 p.m. Call (843) 522-1866 or go to emilysrestaurant.com for reservations.

The **Two-Suns Inn** at 1705 Bay St. is a restored Neoclassical Revival–style home that once served as a residence for female teachers living and working here in Beaufort. Today it is a bed-and-breakfast with some of the best bay views in town. Rates are $150 per night and up. Call (843) 522-1122 or visit twosunsinn.com.

Four or five blocks away at 910 Bay St. is **Luther's,** in the old Luther's Pharmacy building. The staff here call the place "the fun spot on the waterfront" and recommend you show up in shorts or jeans. Luther's serves hot dogs, homemade potato chips, eight different kinds of sandwiches, and nine kinds of half-pound burgers. If you're in the mood, you can order steak, ribs, or fresh shrimp. All meals are served with homemade bread. Prices range from $10 to $25. It's a great place to eat and linger and watch the locals watching the tourists and the tourists watching the locals. Open 11 a.m. to 10 p.m. (later on weekends), seven days a week. The restaurant features live entertainment Thurs through Sun. Call (843) 521-1888.

If you drive a few miles down Bay Street, you'll see the signs to *Parris Island*—follow them. Unlike most military bases, which discourage visitors, this active Marine Corps base welcomes them. Visitors may take a driving tour of the island; the tour leads through the old navy yard and to the site of the Spanish forts that were here in the 17th century. You can also visit the War Memorial Building on the base, where you can see exhibits on the history and development of Parris Island and the history of the Marine Corps. The island is open year-round, Mon through Fri from 7 a.m. to 4:30 p.m. and on Sat, Sun, and holidays from 9 a.m. to 4:30 p.m. Call (843) 525-2951. For general information, visit mcrdpi.usmc.mil.

Just outside of town in Beaufort Town Center, *The Beaufort Bookstore* at 2127 Boundary St. is the largest independent bookstore around and sells current books and bestsellers. Local books, local recipes, and the famous ghost books for which the area is known can be found here, too. They also have a good supply of my novels and short stories. Call (843) 525-1066 or go to beaufortbookssc.com.

Leave Beaufort and head out over the Lady's Island Bridge for *Fripp Island,* about 25 miles away. The islands get confusing here—Lady's, Pritchards, Hunting, and then Fripp all stem off Highway 21. Just follow the signs and you can't go wrong.

Gullah Country

Heading for the end of Fripp Island on Highway 21, you'll pass through the tiny village of *St. Helena Island,* which is probably the center of the Gullah culture and language. These inhabitants of the South Carolina coast are the only group of African Americans who have been able to trace their roots to the villages of the Sierra Leone territory in West Africa. This heritage is evidenced most dramatically in the rice agriculture, cast-net fishing, and arts and crafts such as the coiled basketry of these lowlands, as well as the language and the music.

A half mile from the center of St. Helena Island is the ***Penn Center Historic District.*** This was the first school established in the South to educate the freed slaves. The center has 19 buildings, including cottages for groups of up to 100, and a small museum dedicated to the language and culture of the blacks who were native to this region. Penn Center was designated a National Historic Landmark in 1974. For information on the events that take place here, visit penncenter.com or call (843) 838-2432. Or, write to Penn Center Historic District, PO Box 126, St. Helena Island 29920. The museum is open Mon through Sat from 11 a.m. until 4 p.m. Admission is $3 for children and $5 for adults.

On Highway 21 in the middle of St. Helena Island, you'll find the ***Red Piano Too Art Gallery.*** It's impossible to miss and is certainly the most interesting art gallery in the entire Southeast. The building, for years a big grocery store, is a high-ceilinged wooden structure that has been on the National Register of Historic Places for some years now and is a one-of-a-kind masterpiece. Red Piano Too exhibits and sells African-American artwork that ranges in price from $5 to $1,500. Much of the work is done locally, and the imagination and craftsmanship are truly remarkable. A couple of the artists represented here are "Missionary" Mary Proctor and Red Beans & Nice, and their work is just as interesting as their names. Red Piano Too also sells postcards, prints, Bibles written in Gullah, and small hand-painted memorabilia. The gallery even has a Pat Conroy Room where all of his books (autographed) are sold. If you are in Beaufort, or near Beaufort, or anywhere in South Carolina, this is a place you have to see. Their address is 870 Sea Island Pkwy., St. Helena 29920. Call (843) 838-2241 or see more at redpianotoo.com.

Continuing on toward Fripp Island on Highway 21, try the ***Shrimp Shack,*** 1925 Sea Island Pkwy., which features casual family dining on an outside porch. Prices here are in anybody's ballpark. For about $10 you get a fried or boiled shrimp dinner with sides of red rice and coleslaw along with a Low Country hush puppy, which is a deep-fried corn stick shaped like a torpedo. The name goes back to the time when the kitchens to the plantations were in the backyards, and the cooks would toss corn bread to the yapping dogs and say, "Hush now, puppy." No reservations are necessary, but if you want to call ahead for a take-out order, call (843) 838-2962. They are open for lunch Mon through Sat, and payment is by cash only.

Gullah-n-Geechie Mahn Tours offers packages for bus tours as well as private van tours of the islands, where the Gullah culture is most apparent. You may choose tours that concentrate on such areas of interest as Gullah/Low Country cuisine (Low Country boil or oyster roast); cultural performances featuring storytelling unique to the Gullah culture, dance performances, plantation melodies, blues, and jazz; and crafts and demonstrations that include sweetgrass basket weaving, crabbing, shrimping, and net making. They will also make arrangements for your overnight accommodations, fishing, boat rides, and beach and shopping excursions, as well as golf and tennis games. Call (843) 838-7516 or (843) 838-6312 for tour arrangements; write to PO Box 1248, St. Helena Island 29920; or visit them at gullahngeechietours.net.

Still on Highway 21 heading for Fripp Island, stop at *Gay Fish Company,* 1948 Sea Island Pkwy., for fresh shrimp and fish by the pound or the hundredweight. Charlie Gay also sells spices for cooking shrimp, cookbooks, and marine supplies. More than a dozen shrimp boats dock at the pier here, and Charlie says if you talk to any of the captains, you will be able to make arrangements to go out on a shrimp run. Call (843) 838-2763. If you want to go, set the alarm clock—the boats leave at 4 a.m.

Continue on Highway 21 toward Fripp Island. This will take you to *Hunting Island State Park,* one of South Carolina's most spectacular parks. Located at one end of the park is the Hunting Island Lighthouse, the only one of the seven South Carolina lighthouses open to the public. The beach here is ideal for shelling. For an incredible view of the entire area, you can take a deep breath and climb the 167 steps to the top of the lighthouse. Reservations can be made for camping and the rental cabin in the park. Write Hunting Island State Park, 2555 Sea Island Parkway, Hunting Island 29920, or call (843) 838-2011. Their website is huntingisland.com.

While parts of this extraordinary, smooth beach are reserved for swimming and surfing, other areas are used by surf anglers. Comfort stations complete with showers are placed in several locations along the beach. The park also provides biking and nature trails. Open year-round from daybreak to dark, with adult admission of $5 and children ages 6 to 15 at $3 (younger than 6 is free).

As far as a lot of us down here in the Carolinas are concerned, the best and most accessible resort on the coast is *Fripp Island Resort.* Not only is it remote enough to qualify as "off the beaten path," it has the perfect geography: a pristine beach on one side and a great sweep of tidal marshland on the other. Since tidal marshland cannot be developed, the resort will never get too big or too commercial or too anything. It's the perfect size. For an affordable resort, Fripp has every amenity the larger resorts have but without the spread and the density and the impersonality that often comes with it. For an idea of what the beach and the live oak and Spanish moss landscape looks like, pick up videos of two movies that were shot here: *Forrest Gump* and Disney's *The Jungle Book.*

When you rent a one-, two-, or three-bedroom condo or a beachfront house here, you automatically become a guest member of the Fripp Island Club and have full access to all of the resort facilities. Included in these are two top-notch golf courses. The latest, at Ocean Creek, was designed by Davis Love III and has been named one of the best new courses in the country by *Golf Magazine.* The resort also provides a "Wee Links" setup on each course. This consists of tee placements for kids where they can play from shorter yardages and still be on a championship course. The advantage here is that your child can play along with you.

Fripp Island Resort, keeping the family in mind, has also provided a children's play pool with an alligator slide and giant frog and a lagoon-style pool with caves and waterfalls. Other facilities include croquet courts, a playground with a pirate ship, a basketball court, tennis facilities, and bike rentals. The tennis facilities are excellent, with eight soft courts and two hard courts. You can also rent skiffs, kayaks, or pontoon boats and take a trip on one of the beautiful creeks and waterways to watch for herons, ospreys, pelicans, and dolphins and explore the marshlands. Fishing tackle and crab and shrimp nets can be rented. Guided wildlife excursions are available for six passengers or fewer.

The food at Fripp Island Resort ranges from excellent Low Country seafood and sizzling steaks served at the ***Ocean Point Grille Restaurant*** overlooking the ocean to hot dogs and ice cream at the sides of the three Olympic-size pools.

For the family that wants to live on or near the beach and wants to play golf or tennis, fish, crab, swim, and investigate the wildlife in a truly spectacular setting, Fripp Island Resort is where you should be. Since the rates vary with the season and what kind of rental you are looking for, you should contact the resort for current rates. Write Fripp Island Resort, 201 Tarpon Blvd., Fripp Island 29920, or call (888) 741-8974. You can also visit frippislandresort.com.

Fripp Island Marina is located out on the end of Highway 21 on Fripp Island at 28 Salt Wind Dr., St. Helena Island. Here you can fish from the 27-foot *Glory Halleluyah II,* which can accommodate up to six guests. Captain Eddie supplies bait, tackle, ice, and all the instructions you need to make your trip first-class. His Pro-Line Sportfisherman is fully equipped with the latest electronics, head, icebox, stereo, and full cabin. He specializes in trolling for mackerel, kingfish, amberjack, bonito, barracuda, cobia, dolphin, wahoo, and sailfish. A full day offshore is priced at $880, a three-quarter day is $680, and a half day is $480. If you haven't tried this, it's a real thrill. Just bring sunblock and wear soft-soled shoes. Call (843) 838-3782. For more on the marina events or navigational directions there, visit frippislandresort.com/marina.

From Fripp Island Marina go back through Beaufort on Highway 21. As you leave Beaufort, the kids will enjoy stopping to climb upon and take pictures of the three jet fighters poised for flight at the gates of the **Marine Corps Air Station.**

Sheldon Church Ruins, on Highway 21 near Gardens Corner, is something truly off the beaten path. It's a beautiful old brick Episcopal church set in the middle of three or four huge live oaks with a cemetery at the side and in the back with tombstones dating back before 1700. The old church has been burned two times and during the last 150 years has not even had a roof. But the simple brick columns still reach up and up into the Spanish moss, and the altar and front facade, highlighted with the sun streaming through the leaves, give it a grace and dignity that require nothing else. No surprise that this is a popular spot for picnics and also weddings. An annual service is held here the second Sunday after Easter; if you're within 100 miles, drive over—it will be an experience you will never forget.

Farther out Highway 21, just before you hit I-95, are two spots the kids will like. The first is **Pocotaligo,** which is the smallest town in the state. As reported earlier, the name is a short version of "poke a turtle's tail and he will go." The town is so small, it has only one sign and the last population count was fewer than 12. Natives joke that it's more of a place than a town. Tourists coming through often stop and back up to take a photograph of the sign.

Nearby is **Hobo Joe's,** which is next door to **Sad Sam's,** which is across the road from **Jolly Joe's.** Together, all three of these places look like a series of sideshows at a carnival. But they're not. This is the way we merchandise fireworks down here in the "hard lard belt." At any one of these places, you can buy anything from penny firecrackers to bottle rockets to $50 10-stage Roman candles that go as high as 500 feet. You can even buy $100 extravaganzas that fire 100 salvos and end with a Fourth of July celebration that looks not unlike the New York City fireworks on the East River. This will be a great treat for the kids because South Carolina law allows you to take them out in any uninhabited field and fire away. Everybody does it. So get plenty of punk for lighting your explosives and have fun. ***Caution:*** Be sure to use long sticks of punk to light fireworks, and make sure the fuse is sticking straight out. And don't hold exploding Roman candles.

Hilton Head

The resident Indians here on Hilton Head fought off the settlements of the Spanish, the French, and the British until the middle of the 1700s. At that time they finally were overwhelmed by the British, who took over the area; introduced indigo, cotton, and rice; and started what was to become a boom economy that lasted until after the Civil War. Much hand labor was used to turn the leaves of the indigo plant in the cakes of blue dye that were in great demand at this time all around the world. Part of that labor involved stirring the steaming vats of foul-smelling indigo with long paddles. Slaves were imported from Barbados and later from Africa to accomplish this task and many others. When the slaves were freed after the Civil War, the planters left the island to them and went back to Charleston and inland to the Upcountry of South Carolina. The freed slaves now owned and worked the land and developed the Gullah culture with its own language, which is a mix of English, African dialects, and Calypso-sounding French. It is wonderful to listen to once you get the hang and rhythm of it.

In the 20th century the island's climate and beautiful beaches began attracting developers, who began buying land on the island. Slowly but inexorably the blacks with their rich Gullah tradition were forced to leave the land. Many of them work today in service jobs on Hilton Head Island, and a few own small businesses there, but many have moved to the mainland around Bluffton. Luckily much of the Gullah tradition is still present here and can be seen in the Low Country cuisine, arts, music, and language.

Today Hilton Head has much to offer the tourist. The main attractions are the greatest concentration of outstanding golf courses, tennis facilities, fishing marinas, and accommodations in the country. All 25 golf courses are on the big island and neighboring Daufuskie Island. A few courses are private and thus for members only, but most are available for guests of the hotels and villas.

The winters here are very mild, but the ocean water is still very cold. You can't go swimming in the ocean, unless you only do it for a very few seconds, but you can play golf and tennis, ride bikes, take nature walks, and go sailing and deep-sea fishing.

The **RBC Heritage Golf Tournament** in mid-April is internationally famous and is played on the weekend after the Masters Tournament in Augusta, Georgia, right across the South Carolina border. Tickets for the Heritage are usually available, and it is one of those rare tournaments where you can actually walk right along the course with your favorite professional. See rbcheritage.com.

Palmetto Dunes is perhaps the ideal spot on Hilton Head to bring a sports-minded family. This 2,000-acre resort has three championship golf courses, the nationally acclaimed Palmetto Dunes Tennis Center, a deepwater marina, and more than 3 miles of uninterrupted beach. Uninterrupted here means that sometimes you won't see a single soul for a mile. For reservations and information call (866) 380-1778 or visit their website at palmettodunes.com.

While there is such a thing as a Palmetto Dunes Club private membership, and the feeling is definitely that of a private club, all three courses here and the tennis courts are open year-round to the public. Guests at the **Hilton Head Marriott Resort & Spa** and the **Omni Hilton Head Oceanfront Resort** at Palmetto Dunes are given preferential tee times and reduced rates. Incidentally, these are the golf courses former president Bill Clinton played every spring when he came to the island for the Renaissance Convention.

Doug Weaver, one of the best pros to play on the PGA Tour, is now in residence at Palmetto Dunes, where he gives group lessons. Doug has won some of the biggest tournaments in the country, and today he is rated with the best of the best as an instructor of the game. He feels that amateurs' main problems stem from their setup, grip, and stance, and he believes every lesson should begin by working on these basics. Doug is excellent in short-game management and thinks the basic chip and run should be a great deal like the putting stroke. He also believes in changing amateurs' basic swing as little as possible and trying to get them to believe in tempo and balance. Rates range from $70 to $120 for a 50-minute private lesson; clinics for kids 12 and older are $25. Call (843) 785-1138 for more details. For more on Hilton Head Island golf, go to hiltonheadgolf.com.

While the Marriott Resort & Spa and the Omni Oceanfront Resort are stunning places to stay, many prefer the more informal villas, which are ideal for families. The villas as a group are like a giant two-story hotel spread around 25 pools; the result is that every three or four villas have semiprivate swimming. You can rent a two- or three-bedroom villa facing the tennis courts, one of the golf courses, or the ocean. You can even rent one on a stream with a free canoe tossed in. If you have enough scout merit badges, you can pack your golf clubs or tennis racket carefully in the middle of the canoe and paddle to the course or the court. The villas come equipped with wonderful kitchens; supermarket shopping is less than a mile away. If you're traveling with children, you can use the babysitting and day-care facilities here, and if the kids are turned loose on the ocean or at one of the pools, there are plenty of well-trained lifeguards. The villas offer a unique combination of privacy and convenience to the golf courses, tennis courts, supermarkets, and a mall of outlet stores.

While Hilton Head may appear to be crowded in the high season—spring and fall—Palmetto Dunes is set way back from the main road, and the traffic is completely off the beaten path. As a result, the resort offers as much isolation as you want. Alligators up to 14 feet long thrive among the creeks and lakes here, as do raccoons, deer, and an occasional red fox. In the evening, possums pad from one house to the next looking for handouts. If you stand still long enough at night, there's a good chance of seeing one of the four or five native owls. Bird-watching here is like no place in the country. Audubon Society members, who visit often, have recorded more than 120 species in the immediate area. Watch for the painted bunting, the indigo bunting, the osprey, and the black skimmer, who glides along flashing its red bill to attract the fish, then makes a 180-degree turn and comes back and scoops them up with the lower part of its bill. These birds only operate when the water is calm. But watch for them—they're out there.

Harbour Town, located around the rim of Calibogue Sound, is dominated by the candy-striped **Hilton Head Lighthouse.** The cove, with its 90-odd-slip yacht basin, is home for the serious boaters who travel the Intracoastal Waterway. A pleasant pastime here is to sit on one of the many rocking chairs with a drink or an ice-cream cone or nothing and watch the boats coming in as the sun sets. If you've watched the Heritage Classic Golf Tournament on television, this area will look familiar. Surrounding the cove is a series of upscale shops, restaurants, and condominiums.

Directly across from the cove is **The Harbour Town Grill,** located in the clubhouse of the Harbour Town Golf Links. This small grill looks out over the ninth hole of the course and the putting green. The grill is open daily for breakfast, lunch, and dinner. Call (843) 363-8380 for reservations. Also near the lighthouse in Harbour Town is the fashionable **CQ's Restaurant,** at 140 Lighthouse Rd., which is open nightly from 5 to 9:30 p.m. Call (843) 671-2779. Their website is cqsrestaurant.com.

Back on US 278 at the gateway to Hilton Head is the **Tanger Outlet Mall,** 1414 Fording, Bluffton. This mall, with dozens of name-brand merchants, is the area's largest outlet shopping center. Some of the brands are Eddie Bauer, J. Crew, and Polo. Call (843) 837-5410. A full list of the outlet stores is at tangeroutlet.com.

When you tire of golf and shopping, head for **Reilley's Grill and Bar,** 7D Greenwood Dr., Hilton Head Plaza. Very popular for lunch and dinner, it's a combination grill, bar, sports bar, and hangout. Several televisions are always honed in on whatever sports event is in the air. Hamburgers and fries are especially good here, as are the coffee and desserts. The average lunch will cost you about $10; you can spend more for dinner, but try the burger first. The waitresses are friendly and funny. This is a great place to have a beer and watch the local action. There's a very good chance you'll come back. Open seven days a week from 11 a.m. to 10 p.m. (the bar is open later). Call (843) 842-4414.

A few words about alligators on Hilton Head and all over the Low Country. I played golf here with a comic named Kenny Davis who had never been north of Tahoe or east of Vegas. He had never been to a zoo, and the only alligators he had ever seen were in the movies. I told him I could guarantee that he would see at least a dozen when we played golf on Hilton Head.

Well, we teed off, and perhaps the cloud cover was too thick or too thin or the pollen count was wrong, but for some reason we didn't see a single gator—only egrets, pelicans, doves, and an occasional pileated woodpecker. Finally, on the 17th hole, long after Kenny had decided that there was no such thing as an alligator, there beside a lagoon lay a monster that looked longer than my Ford.

Kenny looked at it and began laughing. It was so big and looked so ridiculous and so asleep, he thought it was something plastic up from Disney World that I'd had some redneck buddy blow up for his benefit. Before I could stop him, he was prodding the beast with his putter. And then two strange events happened simultaneously: The alligator's mouth opened, and the monster rose up in a hissing, rushing lunge. Kenny did a quickstep and levitated 2 or 3 feet, straight up. He did some aerial acrobatics, hit the ground running, and didn't turn around until he was 100 yards down the fairway. He was no longer laughing. Yes, Virginia, there are alligators down here.

Places to Stay in the Southern Corner

BEAUFORT

Beaufort Inn
809 Port Republic St.
(843) 379-4667
beaufortinn.com

Cuthbert House Inn
1203 Bay St.
(843) 521-1315
cuthberthouseinn.com

Two-Suns Inn
1705 Bay St.
(843) 522-1122
twosunsinn.com

Places to Eat in the Southern Corner

BEAUFORT

Emily's
906 Port Republic St.
(843) 522-1866
emilysrestaurant.com

Rhett House Inn
1009 Craven St.
(843) 524-9030
rhetthouseinn.com

EDISTO ISLAND

Old Post Office Restaurant
1442 Highway 174
(843) 869-2339
theoldpostofficerestaurant.com

The Pavilion Restaurant
102 Palmetto Blvd.
(843) 869-4474

ST. HELENA ISLAND

Shrimp Shack
1925 Sea Island Pkwy.
(843) 838-2962

THE GRAND STRAND

Fishing Villages & Wildlife Refuges

After leaving the civilized city of Charleston, you return to the tidal marshland Low Country landscape you have come to know well. Along the coastline north of Greater Charleston, the land stays about the same as in the Southern Corner for about 100 miles: sandy beaches, barrier islands, and thick swampland. Then around Surfside and northward the islands begin to thin out and a great wide beach, known as the Grand Strand, takes over and continues all the way to the North Carolina line.

Forty miles north of Charleston on Highway 17, the tiny village of *McClellanville* has sat peacefully under the live oaks along Jeremy Creek for the past 200 years. This quaint little commercial fishing village came into national prominence in late September of 1989 when the full brunt of Hurricane Hugo hit here and destroyed or damaged every standing structure. At the height of the storm most of the citizens of McClellanville, who thought they were safe inside the brand-new Lincoln High School, were playing cards by flashlight, listening to their radios, and sleeping. Suddenly the storm punched out 13 air-conditioner casements, and water cascaded down the halls and into the rooms. Inside the cafeteria/auditorium where 1,200 people were gathered, the water quickly reached the incredible height of 6 feet, 1 inch. To save themselves from drowning, the men, women, and children climbed up on desks, tables, and chairs and the small stage at the end of the big room. Many men and women, standing on chairs standing on tables, punched out ceiling panels and placed their children up on the thin metal support beams, where they stayed until the storm finally stopped around 3 in the morning.

One teacher in charge of a group of infants and some elderly people on the far side of the building thought she would spend the night high and dry in her small classroom. But when she looked outside through the glass-partitioned steel door, she almost had a heart attack. Before her very eyes, shrimp and fish were swimming by. The water outside the building had risen to more than 10 feet. Quickly she led her charges down the dark halls to the cafeteria only to face the unbelievable sight of the fast-rising water.

TOP RECOMMENDATIONS IN THE GRAND STRAND

Brookgreen Gardens
Highway 17 at Murrells Inlet
1931 Brookgreen Dr.
Murrells Inlet
(843) 235-6000
brookgreen.org

Georgetown Ice Company
330 N. Fraser St.
Georgetown
(843) 546-6169

House of Blues
4640 Highway 17 South
North Myrtle Beach
(843) 272-3000
houseofblues.com

Tidewater Golf Club and Plantation
1400 Tidewater Dr.
North Myrtle Beach
(843) 913-2424
tidewatergolf.com

Yawkey Wildlife Center
1 Yawkey Way South
Georgetown
(843) 546-9559
dnr.sc.gov/mlands

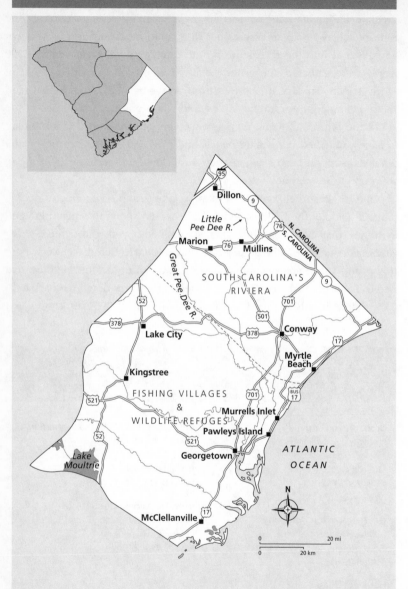

Miraculously the water stopped rising at the 6-foot, 1-inch level. Even more miraculously, no one was injured.

It took McClellanville more than five years to rebuild, but the marks that Hugo left behind will be here forever. At **Lincoln High School,** a bronze plaque at the entrance to the cafeteria shows where the water crested. If you would like to see Lincoln High School and the high-water mark in the cafeteria, and maybe hear some more Hugo stories, turn left on Dupre to Lincoln Road. The school will be right in front of you. Most of the school's current faculty was here the night Hugo struck; everyone has a fascinating story.

The **McClellanville United Methodist Church** on the corner of Pinckney and Dupre is ideal for a photograph if you step back far enough and get a shot through the live oaks when the sun and shadows are right. Another block away is the brown-shingled **St. James Episcopal Church,** which is also surrounded by live oaks. The last time I was here, at least a dozen mockingbirds were up in the trees. If you're from anywhere north of Yonkers and have trouble identifying mockingbirds, just look for the sergeant's stripes on their wings. You can also whistle a three-, four-, or five-note tune and, if you're lucky and they're in the right mood, they'll play it back for you.

Nearby is the tiny village of **Awendaw,** which was also leveled by Hugo. Oysters from here and nearby **Bulls Bay** are famous all over South Carolina. The village owes much of its livelihood to their preparation for shipping.

Sewee Bay, a mile or so away, was named for an Indian tribe, and on its shores are numerous mounds of refuse and broken pottery from their prehistoric dwellings. After the white settlers came, the Sewee Indians felt that the English were not giving them a fair deal, so they planned to seek the English king and personally lay their grievances before him. Building huge canoes, they sailed into the open sea and were never heard from again. A pirate captured soon after the Indians' disappearance swore that he had seen the canoes far out in the Atlantic.

Not to be confused with the Sewee war party that struck out for England, the **Seewee Restaurant,** back down the road on Highway 17, is probably the finest spot on the coastline for fresh seafood. The phone number is (843) 928-3609, and the hours are generally from 11 a.m. to 9 p.m. Mon through Fri, 8 a.m. to 10 p.m. Sat, and 11 a.m. to 3 p.m. Sun. Prices for lunch start at $8.95 and go up to $18.95. The delicious dinners range from $8.95 to $29.95. Because Seewee is only a few miles from McClellanville, they get all of their shrimp, soft-shell crabs, and flounder right off the boat. In other words, this is fresh seafood that really means fresh. You might even enjoy going to the McClellanville docks, watching the boats come in, and then taking the pleasant ride back through the old fishing town that Hugo almost destroyed but is now back up to speed.

Close by on Highway 17—you'll have to watch for the signs—is **Hampton Plantation.** Set back from the road on a 2.5-mile drive, this is one of the finest examples of antebellum architecture in the entire South. When Henry Middleton Rutledge departed Hampton to serve the Confederacy during the Civil War, he left behind one of the grandest homes and most prosperous agricultural enterprises in America. The decades before the Civil War witnessed the high point of rice cultivation in South Carolina, and Hampton Plantation was one of the leaders. At this time Hampton was using the daily action of the tides on the freshwater rivers to irrigate the fields.

When Colonel Rutledge returned to Hampton Plantation in 1865, he returned to an entirely different South, one in which Hampton Plantation would never again hold the position it once had as a center of political and economic life in the state. The grand house remained unpainted and in decay; cotton was stored in the grand ballroom; crops were planted among the live oaks on the once stately lawn. By 1923 both the colonel and his wife were dead, and the house stood abandoned.

The colonel's son, Archibald Hamilton Rutledge—outdoorsman, writer, and the first poet laureate of South Carolina—returned to Hampton from teaching school in Pennsylvania and at age 56 began a long process of renovating the mansion. He described his labor of love in his best-known book, *Home by the River:* "When I first came back, it was sagging in places and it had not been painted in a generation. Now everything has been done to restore it without changing it and it gleams under its four coats of white paint. It is no unusual thing for visitors to tell me that in its simple dignity it is the most impressive home they have ever seen."

Now protected under the auspices of **Hampton Plantation State Park,** 1950 Rutledge Rd., the mansion may be opened by appointment or rented for special occasions. A guided tour of the house, the grounds, and the nature trails surrounding the mansion can be arranged by calling (843) 546-9361. The park itself is open daily year-round from 9 a.m. to 5 p.m., with free admission to the grounds. The mansion is open year-round Sat through Tues, with guided tours only at 1, 2, and 3 p.m. It is closed Wed through Fri. A fee of $7.50 for adults and $3.50 for ages 6 to 15 is charged for admission to the mansion. Of the several related websites, I think the best is south-carolina-plantations.com/charleston/hampton.html. You can also visit southcarolinaparks.com/hampton.

While this plantation is truly one of the great sights of this part of the country, the unsuspecting traveler must be warned of a little item down here that can cause considerable discomfort—the deerfly. This noxious little beast can reduce a full-grown man or woman to quivering suet in minutes. Be prepared by picking up an insect repellent from Buster Brown back in McClellanville. Long-sleeved shirts are also advised. Travel tip: The deerfly is not confined to the Hampton Estates—it is literally everywhere down here. Also abundant are the "no-see-ums," aka gnats. In any case, insect repellent and long-sleeved shirts will solve what could be a terrible problem.

A friend of mine interviewed a 110-year-old gentleman not too long ago and posed the question of what was the most important single invention he had witnessed in the century behind him. The old man counted on his fingers: the automobile, the airplane, the atomic bomb, landing on the moon, and the computer. Then he said, "Now these are all very fine, but you know something, if I've got to go with the one that's the most important for me, I've got to go with screens."

And while you're in the neighborhood of Hampton Plantation, it is worthwhile to make another off-the-beaten-path stop at **St. James–Santee Church** (The Brick Church), about a mile on down the road from Hampton, then turn left on the sandy road—that is, if it hasn't rained lately. Back in George Washington's day, it would have been *on* the beaten path since this sandy path was part of the King's Highway running north and south during colonial times. In fact, George even passed through here on his presidential tour through the southern states in 1791. Now it is virtual wilderness, which makes the St. James–Santee Church and its small but architecturally important presence even more of a surprise. The church has two classical porticos, each supported by four brick Doric columns. If you're lucky, and the church is open, you can see the high-backed boxed pews which have never been painted and the vaulted ceiling which retains the original plaster dating from 1768. This precious gem was one of the Anglican chapels of ease originally built to make it "easy" for the area plantation owners to worship and tithe in their rural settings. For more about the history of this fascinating church, visit stjamesec.org or call (843) 887-4386.

On up Highway 17, 1.5 miles north of Georgetown, turn off at the sign for **Hobcaw Barony** and go to the **Discovery Center** at the right of the gate, at 22 Hobcaw Rd. The modern history of Hobcaw Barony began at the turn of the century. In the winter of 1905, New York financier Bernard Baruch acquired all of the land that once made up 10 rice plantations. Hobcaw's tranquil woods and waters provided Baruch with recreation and relief from the pressures of public life. Baruch shared the peaceful world of Hobcaw with his family, friends, and many distinguished associates, including Sir Winston Churchill and President Franklin Delano Roosevelt. In the old mansion you can see photographs of Baruch on various hunting trips as well as shots of him with Churchill and Roosevelt. The barony includes about 9,000 acres of tidal wetlands, oyster reefs, former rice fields, and waterways on or bordering the Belle W. Baruch Foundation's 17,500-acre wildlife refuge. Belle Baruch, Bernard Baruch's daughter, worked diligently to preserve the barony for ecological research by creating the foundation prior to her death in 1964.

The Discovery Center at the entrance to the estate has wonderful exhibits of Low Country animals and plants. The kids will be especially delighted with the live baby alligator, but for goodness' sake, don't touch it! At this wildlife refuge you can collect enough wildlife information to last a lifetime. A sample of the seminars (some are free) include "A Land Ethic for Our Time" and "Native Spirit, The Waccamaw Indian People." Wildlife trips include "Birding on the Barony." The course blurb reads, "Join Naturalist Jerry Walls as he conducts professional guided birding & nature tours throughout the property. Dozens of species of birds can be located throughout Hobcaw Barony. Possible bird species include bald eagles, ospreys, painted buntings, endangered red-cockaded woodpeckers, shorebirds, wading birds & more." The three-hour Hobcaw Barony tour is limited to 20 people; the fee is $20. Other tours originating from the Hobcaw Barony Discovery Center are "Hobcaw Flyfishing Adventure," "Hobcaw Barony Photo

Safari," and "Trail Ride with Your Own Horse." Learn more at hobcawbarony
.org or call (843) 546-4623.

If you're hungry and heading north on Highway 17 (just south of Pawleys Island), watch on the left side of the road for the sign for **Hog Heaven.**
There's no address here, but if you miss it, you can make a U-turn and go
back. The old owner, George Young, used to say, "Some people on the road
smell the smoke and make the turn and come back." Hog Heaven, formerly
Yum's Barbeque, has the finest pork barbecue on the Eastern Seaboard.
Hours are 11:30 a.m. to 9 p.m. daily. Prices range from $4.75 to $15. There's
more on Hog Heaven at hogheaveninc.com, or call (843) 237-PIGG.

On Barbecue

When you arrive in the Palmetto State, you are in the official Tigris and Euphrates
land of barbecue. Right down in here is where it all began. You have probably
heard how Texas claims they have the best. Well, we shall now put that myth
to rest. The Lone Star State, while it may have many wonderful things, does not
have hickory wood. Without hickory wood you cannot have true barbecue. Now,
they may call what they serve barbecue, because it's a free country, and they can
call anything they cook, serve, and eat anything they want. But around here, if
you mention Texas barbecue, someone's going to drift out to the parking lot and
check your license plates.

Down here in the "hard lard belt," our barbecue is cooked with hickory wood and
hickory wood only, and the sauce is either mustard based or vinegar and pepper
based. And that is the long and the short of it. North Carolina has hickory wood,
and they have on occasion been known to produce a good three rib down cross-
breed hog. But your basic North Carolinians do not have good sense, because
they will drench down that pork with ketchup-based sauce and that will not do it.

As far as I'm concerned—and I have been a judge on many barbecue contests
and do not treat it lightly—South Carolina barbecue is, and always has been, light
years ahead of the rest of the country. Using smaller hogs—the three rib down
category—and hickory wood and hickory coals, our barbecue will cross the finish line as tender as pound cake, and with our sauces and white loaf bread and
coleslaw and cold beer or lemonade, it will drop you to your knees, where you
will weep tears of appreciation and never-ending gratitude. At the Springfield Frog
Jump, the Irmo Okra Strut, and the Salley Chitlin Strut, I have seen serious men in
business suits and full-grown Christian women go into what is called a "barbecue
coma." So much for barbecue.

Highway 17 runs right through the heart of **Georgetown.** This is the third-oldest city in South Carolina and is named after King George II. The entire district, which lies along the Sampit River and the white settlement of which dates back to the 1700s, is listed on the National Register of Historic Places. Long before the Revolutionary War, most of the wealth of the town came from indigo; later it came from rice. Today the two main industries are steel and paper production, but the old, deep harbor is still an important shipping port.

The **Red Store–Tarbox Warehouse** (very early 18th century) is a good spot to start your tour of this fascinating town. Originally this was part of a three-story brick tavern that also stored silks, indigo, and imported wines, as well as mail from English ships. The glamorous Theodosia Burr Allston, daughter of Aaron Burr, sailed from this wharf in 1812 and was never seen again. Her husband, the governor of South Carolina, died of grief, or so the story goes.

Harborwalk is a 1,000-foot-long, 12-foot-wide boardwalk at the edge of the Sampit River. Along this walk are the back-door entrances and pastel awnings of the Front Street shops and restaurants. This is a delightful place to stroll and get your bearings. Three of the restaurants on Front Street look out over the boardwalk and water. The **River Room** at 801 Front is known for its excellent seafood salads, homemade french-fried onion rings, and its iced tea served in wide-mouthed Mason jars. Prices range from $8 to $12 for lunch. Dinner prices are $10 to $30. Call (843) 527-4110 or visit riverroom georgetown.com.

Also on Front Street—you can't miss it—is the **Town Clock/Old Market** at 633 Front St. Built in 1835, this tower was used as a marketplace, city hall, and lockup. Today it houses the **Rice Museum** on the second floor. It displays the history of the rice empire that flourished here in the 19th century. Admission is $7 for adults, $5 for seniors, $3 for students ages 6 to 21, and free for children under 6 who are accompanied by an adult. Call (843) 546-7423 or check out ricemuseum.org.

Across the street is the **Georgetown County Chamber of Commerce** at 531 Front St. This is also a good spot to start a tour of the older sections of town. Here you can get maps, tourist information, schedules, and a list of bed-and-breakfasts in the area. Call (843) 546-8436 or visit georgetown countychamber.com.

Be sure to pick up a Georgetown National Register Historic District Map. Since there are 62 historic sites all within a comfortable walking distance, I'd suggest simply starting off from the chamber with the map in your hand and following the numbers. Some truly delightful houses are on this walking tour.

A typical house on the tour is the **Harold Kaminski House** at 1003 Front St. Among those who lived here was Confederate Captain Thomas Daggett, a local hero who built the mine that sank the Union flagship *Harvest Moon* in Winyah Bay in 1865. Today the house has an outstanding collection of antiques from various periods. Call (843) 546-7706.

Georgetown Ice Company, 330 N. Fraser St., a low, rambling filling station that has, over the years, turned into the biggest convenience store in the state, is a one-of-a-kind South Carolina wonder. Drop by for a beer or a Blenheim Ginger Ale. This store caters to anglers, hunters, and anyone and everyone passing through. They sell everything, and you'll be hard-pressed to name something they don't have. The range is incredible: fishing rods, tackle, worms, crickets, minnows, hot dogs, clothing, magazines, gas, oil, groceries, pharmaceuticals, boiled peanuts, et cetera, et cetera, et cetera. If you're from the north country, give boiled peanuts a chance. They'll seem vile at first, but they will definitely grow on you. Every time I go to New York City, my friends there beg me to bring them a few large sacks. Call (843) 546-6169 if you want to, but there's no need to phone: They are open 24 hours a day, seven days a week.

The best bet for lodging downtown in the historic district is the **Harbor House Bed and Breakfast** at 15 Cannon St. All the rooms have spectacular harbor views. The house, circa 1765, has been beautifully restored, showcasing its original heart pine floors, colonial decorative moldings, eight fireplaces, and family antiques. Each of the rooms has a private bath, cable TV, and Wi-Fi, and a full breakfast is included, with scrumptious shrimp and grits or sweet potato pancakes often on the menu. Rates vary from $169 to $199 per night. Call (843) 546-6532 or book your room online at harborhousebb.com.

Down on Front Street at 703 is **Thomas's Cafe,** whose a la carte breakfast items can't be beat. Corned beef hash and smoked sausage are $2.25 each; an egg is 80 cents and a biscuit is 75 cents. You get the idea—you can build your own breakfast for under $5. Their lunch prices are pretty appealing, too. The atmosphere is also a step back in time. Their phone number is (843) 546-7776.

Blackwater Adventures is headed by Louis Nexsen, a native with more than 20 years' experience in guiding people through the rivers and inlets in this area. Louis is strongly behind preserving and promoting the natural environment of South Carolina. He offers a trip called *"Black Mingo Creek,"* a half-day (three hours) or full-day (six hours) kayak trip on this secluded stream where General Francis Marion evaded the British during the Revolution. The tour has an option of riverside lodging for an additional charge, with skeet shooting for evening entertainment. The trip costs $65 for adults for the full day and $45 for the half day; lunch is an additional $10 Another trip, the *"Pinopolis Dam Lock System Tour,"* allows you to see the largest single-step dam lock in the world, with a drop of 75 feet. Through the Santee Cooper Lake System (which were the largest artificial lakes in the world until the Aswan Dam was completed), this guided canoe trip provides some unforgettable scenery. Other exclusive trips and overnights in the area can be made by arrangement. Group discounts are also available. Call (800) 761-1850 for inquiries and reservations. Write them at PO Box 4639, Pinopolis 29469, or visit blackwater adventure.com.

Carolina Safari in Myrtle Beach is as eclectic as its tour founder, Virgil Graham, who is an area native, a naturalist, and a magazine photographer. On the jeep tours of various sites in the Low Country, you will see egrets, bald eagles, alligators, maritime forests, and a variety of ecosystems, including saltwater marshes, cypress swamps, and more. Narrative background on Indian, colonial, and antebellum history is offered along with examples of 300-year-old plantations, Drunken Jack's Island, and visits to other legendary haunts of the Low Country.

The jeeps are genuine, customized safari-style touring vehicles that seat up to 14 people, and each one has a personal guide. Binoculars are provided, stops are frequent and spontaneous, and you can take photos from any seat. Three-hour tours are generally offered daily at a cost of $43 for adults, $38 for ages 13 to 19, and $30 for children 12 and under. Pickup is available at most resorts. Special tours and group rates can be arranged. Call (843) 497-5330 for reservations and further information or visit carolina safari.com.

Andrews Old Town Hall Museum, 14 W. Main St. (no phone), is open Tues and Thurs only, from 11 a.m. to 1 p.m. and 2 to 4 p.m. or by appointment. The museum is located in the town of Andrews, inland 18 miles west of Georgetown on Highway 521. Representing a typical Victorian-era Andrews home, everything in the museum is circa 1909, the year Andrews was founded. Included are a child's room with period toys, a complete kitchen, and a Victorian parlor with period furniture, pictures, a pump organ, and a Victrola. Also depicting 1909 life are a complete Victorian schoolroom and a farm shed with tools, scales, harnesses and traces, hogshead containers, a plow, and plow points For more see lowcountry-sc.com/andrews/oldtown.htm.

North of Georgetown a few miles, you're in ***Pawleys Island*** country. The bumper stickers on the cars of some of the summer inhabitants say ARRO-GANTLY SHABBY. Despite this cloying little observation, the people are friendly and the island is a one-of-a-kind gem. Many of the beach houses have been here since long before the Civil War.

Just staying on Pawleys Island for a week or so is in itself a perfect vacation, but there is much more to do here than just bake in the sun and watch for porpoises. Take fishing, specifically surf fishing. You need no license, and you can fish literally anywhere on the beach where you can cast a line. Surf fishing starts in the spring, and the favorite spots are right here: the south end of Litchfield Beach, the south and north end of Pawleys, and the south end of Garden City Beach. All of these run together, so there's no trouble finding your way. For surf fishing you'll need a surf rod, which you can buy or rent from almost any store in Pawleys. The rod should be between 8 and 11 feet long with an open-face saltwater reel, filled with 10- to 20-pound test monofilament line. You should also have two or three bottom-rig end tackles with 3-ounce pyramid sinkers and 2/0 hooks. You'll need a sand spike to hold your rod, some fresh mullet cut in 1-inch pieces, sunglasses, a cooler filled with your favorite drinks, a beach towel or chair to sit on, and a good book to read.

Why the book? In the spring, three major species of fish are in the surf: sea trout, red drum that have moved out of the estuaries, and bluefish that are moving north along the coast. If any of these fish happen to be feeding, you can get all kinds of action. If the fish haven't arrived at your spot on the beach or have just passed by, you'll have plenty of time to read.

No one really knows what happens when you're sitting in a beach chair with your feet in the water and a surf rod sticking in a sand spike, but it seems that life definitely slows down and down and down. Up and down the endless beach you'll see the young and the old, the fat and the slim, doing it all day, every day. But it's not all just sitting there. Every half hour or so you can rise up, crank in the line, and then cast it out again. Then you can sit back down.

If you enjoy this kind of serenity, stop at **Pawleys Island Supplies,** 10460 Ocean Hwy. (843-237-2912) on Highway 17, rent some equipment, and come on down. You can also check them out at pawleysislandsupplies.com.

If surf fishing and surf sitting aren't dramatic enough for you, you can charter a boat at Georgetown and head out for the Gulf Stream 60 miles away to try your luck with white marlin, blue marlin, dolphin, wahoo, or yellowfin tuna. All fishing tackle and bait are furnished, and you'll have a skilled but expensive captain with radar equipment for spotting the fish and getting you there. The bad news on the price is that it can run as high as $1,200 for the day, and you need at least a week for reservations. The good news is that you can take along five buddies, which comes out to $200 each.

While you're out in the Gulf Stream, the temperature will be hotter (more than 100 degrees), the water will be greener, and you'll see clumps of fern and kelp and whole stalks of coconut trees drifting by from as far away as Barbados. You might fish all day and not get a single strike. But then again you might hook into an 800-pound tarpon or a 400-pound sailfish or find yourself plowing through a school of 200-pound amberjack.

Brookgreen Gardens, a former indigo and rice plantation, is an outdoor sculpture garden located on Highway 17 at Murrells Inlet. It was originally purchased by Archer and Anna Hyatt Huntington as a setting for their art collection. It is now acclaimed as the world's finest collection of American figurative sculpture. If you like the work of Remington, you'll like this. One particular piece will please the kids: a life-size sculpture of an alligator by David Turner. The current total number of pieces in the collection is more than 1,400 works by 340 artists; the collection is still growing. At the entrance is the powerful *Fighting Stallions* by famed sculptress and founder Anna Hyatt Huntington; it is the largest sculpture ever cast in aluminum. This entire garden, with its incredible expanse of grass and beautiful landscape and wildlife, is well worth the visit.

While here, you will also get an idea of how a plantation should look. The 9,127 acres of Brookgreen Gardens extend from the beachfront on the Atlantic Ocean to the freshwater swamps along the Waccamaw River. The garden's paths are laid out in the shape of a butterfly, and flowers bloom here from early spring right into September. The Courtyard Cafe on the grounds overlooks a truly wonderful view of the park and the woods; it serves sandwiches, salads, soups, and snacks. Picnic facilities are located opposite the sculpture gardens' parking lot, next to Jessamine Park. This is the perfect spot for a picnic and is a delightful place to spend several hours. Once again, pack your favorite insect repellent and be prepared for deerflies and no-see-ums. A gift shop here offers gifts, books, and items that tell the story of Brookgreen Gardens. Admission is $14 for adults, $12 for seniors and young adults ages 13 to 18, and $7 for children ages 4 to 12. Admission is good for seven consecutive days. Open daily from 9:30 a.m. to 5 p.m. Call (843) 235-6000 or learn more at brookgreen.org.

Belle Isle and Battery White originally belonged to Revolutionary hero Peter Horry, for whom Horry County is named. Battery White, an earthen Confederate fortification, was built on the plantation overlooking the bay for the defense of Georgetown during the Civil War. A short distance offshore lies the sunken Union flagship *Harvest Moon,* which went down during the last days of Georgetown's Union occupation when a Confederate bomb planted on board went off. The entrance to Belle Isle Yacht Club, now a resort community, is located south of Georgetown off Highway 17 and South Island Road at 1228 Belle Isle Rd. There is no charge to visit Battery White. For access go to the Belle Isle guard gate, which is clearly marked on Highway 17. See batterywhite.org for more information.

Due to the popularity of the **Yawkey Wildlife Center** tour, located at 1 Yawkey Way South in Georgetown, reservations must be made four to six months in advance. Call (843) 546-6814 or go to yawkeyfoundation.org or dnr.sc.gov/mlands. Accessible only by boat, the Yawkey preserve consists of North and South Island and most of Cat Island, three coastal islands at the mouth of Winyah Bay. Willed to the state wildlife department by the late Tom Yawkey, who owned the Boston Red Sox, the center is dedicated to the management of waterfowl habitat. In cooperation with other state agencies, this center was largely responsible for saving the brown pelican a few years back. Today these birds are no longer on the endangered species list.

As a matter of fact, if you're on almost any of the islands down here, you can count as many as 50 or 60 brown pelicans in a single formation as they fly home in the evening.

The Original Hammock Shop, 10880 Ocean Hwy. at Pawleys Island, is open year-round, Mon through Sat from 9:30 a.m. to 6 p.m. and Sun from noon to 5 p.m. Call (843) 237-9122. Since 1978 this has been a favorite destination down here in the Low Country for shoppers. Originally set up to make and sell rope hammocks, they now sell cookbooks, clothing, and beachwear, as well as another hundred items to take home as gifts. One of their most popular items is their famous rope hammocks, which you can see being made right before your eyes. If you want solid comfort and absolutely no danger of falling out, get the wider version, which can accommodate two people or four or five dogs. You can check out their entire catalog at hammockshop.com.

The Original Hammock Shop is located in The Hammock Shops Village which contains another 20 or so specialty shops and eateries in a park-like setting. The charming *Roz's Rice Mill Cafe* specializes in fresh seafood and Low Country cuisine. At *Carolina Gourmet at Pawleys* you can get local and Southern foods. Fill a gift basket here with candy, cookbooks, and gadgets for your chef back home. For a quick bite in between shops, stop in *Island Dogs* for hot dogs and sandwiches with some good ole sweet tea. Finally, *Pawleys Island Mercantile* is truly a wonderful and imaginative clothing and gift store featuring a large selection of outdoor, beach, and resort wear plus accessories, toys, and home decor. And who can resist their candy display? If you want to take a gift to the folks back home, this is probably the best spot to shop on the coast. See thehammockshops.com for more on each of the shops and restaurants in the Village.

Pawleys Island and Litchfield Beaches became, in a real sense, the first resort in America. Some say that malaria-bearing mosquitoes could not fly across the large salt marshes that separated the beaches from the mainland. Pawleys Island in particular became a favorite refuge for wealthy planter families, some of whose houses are still standing today. These planters also built large and lavish houses in Charleston and stayed there during the "social season" of February, which was after the crops were harvested. All the romantic images so often associated with the "Old South" and *Gone with the Wind* grew out of this period.

Fishing: The Party Boat

Of all of the sport-fishing boats that smoke out of Murrells Inlet heading for the Gulf Stream 60 miles out in search of marlin, tuna, and the great white shark, the bottom of the line is the party boat. This is a big iron monster that resembles a locomotive and stretches out 80 to 90 feet, with metal tubes every 18 inches for holding your rods. Standing side by side with another 130 customers, you get the feeling that you are chained together on a slave ship bound for some Dutch possession. Leaving the harbor, the boat throws up a wake so big, other anglers scream and shake their fists. But despite the crowd, and the perfunctory way you are treated, the party boat is the only fishing boat that posts the sign: WE GUARANTEE—YOU WILL CATCH FISH! OR YOUR MONEY BACK!

If you'd like to stay overnight here—and who wouldn't?—stop by **Pawleys Island–Litchfield Business Association** on Highway 17 at The Planter's Exchange. They'll show you a wide range of places to stay, including a 200-year-old beach house, a plantation manor house, bed-and-breakfasts, oceanfront hotel rooms and suites, and rooms and houses on the beach, on the creek, or on one of the many golf courses. For an overview, see hammockcoastsc.com/places-to-stay.

If you ignore the Highway 17 bypass and stay on old Highway 17, you'll go right through the heart of **Murrells Inlet.** Founded in the late 18th century by Captain Murrell, Murrells Inlet has supplied the Waccamaw Neck area with fresh seafood for over 200 years. Fleets of deep-sea fishing boats lie at anchor here and journey daily out to the Gulf Stream to bring back every possible kind of fish for the local restaurants.

Just off Murrells Inlet lies **Drunken Jack's Island,** where, according to local legend, a pirate named Jack was accidentally marooned with no provisions except his shipmates' excess rum supply. Months later, when the ship returned to load up the rum cargo, all the crew found was case after empty case and spent rum bottles all along the shore, plus the bleached bones of poor Jack. The treasure of Blackbeard is also reputed to be buried here.

The highway meanders along under ancient live oaks by many unique seafood restaurants, ranging from old, weathered, time-honored culinary jewels with third-generation chefs and proprietors to more recent dining establishments with troubadours to delight the evening diners.

Perhaps the oldest and best known dining spot is *Lee's Inlet Kitchen,* 4460 Highway 17 Business, Murrells Inlet, where they have been serving fresh fish, shrimp, oysters, scallops, and char-grilled rib eyes and filets since 1948. Everyone I know keeps going back and going back. The third generation of the family continues the tradition of serving only seafood from Carolina shores and loves to hear the stories of patrons who remember sitting in a high chair here only to bring their own children to do the same. They're open Mon through Sat at 4:30 p.m. Call (803) 651-2881 or see lees inletkitchen.com for more.

Nance's Creek Front Restaurant at 4883 Highway 17, Murrells Inlet, has a dining room with at least 100 feet of glass looking out over the marsh and the creek. The view is spectacular because you can see the boats coming in and going out and watch the changing colors on the marsh grass. The food is almost as good as the view. Prices range from $8 to $33. Open Fri through Sun for lunch from 11 a.m. to 2 p.m. Dinner is served daily starting at 4 p.m. Call (843) 651-2696 or take a look at nancescreekfront restaurant.com.

Murrells Inlet is the absolute center for fishing down here. You can fish for almost anything you can imagine. As a matter of fact, the South Carolina coastline, creeks, and inland lakes probably offer a larger variety of fish than any place in the country. The only problem fish are the sharks and stingrays. Swimmers are warned to avoid large schools of fish, for the sharks feed among them. One sign of a shark feeding among fish is the presence of birds, which are waiting to scavenge the scraps.

The stingray is a bottom-dweller in the ocean and salt marshes. It won't attack, but its tail has a clever little barb that can cause a painful wound if it's stepped on. You are cautioned to shuffle your feet when wading in the water, so that they sense you coming and get out of your way. Be on the lookout for jellyfish and Portuguese man-of-wars. If they sting you, a quick remedy is to sprinkle the irritated area with meat tenderizer.

Along with charter-boat fishing for sport fish, there are two other types of fishing, namely, party-boat fishing and pier fishing. On the party boat you will certainly catch fish, but be prepared to put up with a few problems. Beer is sold on board, and, in the hot sun and after a night on the town, a few of your shipmates will be hooked over the rail doing you know what.

To avoid having this happen to you, be sure to eat a very light and very dry breakfast. In other words, leave the grease alone. The trip is long—usually all day. Once the big boat and its typically 100-plus passengers leave the pier, there is no turning back. None, no matter what. On the other hand, it's cheap—around $48 for adults and $30 for children for a half day and around $99 for adults and $65 for children for a full day with rod and reel and bait all thrown in. If you can stand the heat, the captain, who knows the waters and the ways of the fish, will take you places where you can catch something. Children often have a better time here than adults. The largest one of these party boats in South Carolina is operated by Capt. Dick's at 866-557-FISH (3474) or visit captdicks.com.

If you don't want to get on board a party boat, the pier a couple miles north at Surfside is the easiest fishing in the world—and very pleasant. Here you can rent a rod and reel and buy bait, and walk out on the half-mile pier to any seat you like. You cast your line in and sit back and enjoy the breeze. Pier fishers tend to be very agreeable people and will be pleased to answer any questions you have about bait and casting, and they may even identify what you might catch. Since most of the pier is lighted, many anglers come carrying chaise lounges, blankets, coolers of food, and radios and stay all night. For regular daytime fishing, you might catch anything from a blowfish to a shark. With a little luck, you can catch almost anything here if you're patient enough and the weather is right. Try to fish when the tide is coming in, not going out. When it's incoming, the fish follow it in to feed. The only problem you'll have out here if the fish are biting is that the kids will never want to come in.

The **Surfside Pier,** just north of Murrells Inlet, is, at 800 feet, one of the longest fishing piers in the state. It's open 24 hours a day, seven days a week, and is lighted for night fishing. Prices are in the ballpark of $9 to rent a rod and reel, $9 to fish, and $6 for bait. Call the Surfside Pier at (843) 238-0121. Out on the end of the pier, many people fish with big rods and reels and often land spectacular catches. The record here is a 128-pound tarpon that one George Singleton caught out on the end; he wore out a pair of shoes fighting the fish all the way back to the shore.

The Surfside Pier is full of surprise catches. You'll see sand sharks, hammerheads, blowfish, and often a sheepshead as big as a good-size Labrador retriever. Down the middle of the pier are benches, and the old-timers staked out here are usually natives who can and will give you any information you want about the winds and the tides. They'll also be able to identify the strange creatures drawn up from the bottom. The sea robin is of particular interest—it has wings like a bat and a face like a catfish.

Almost everyone likes to talk and give advice down here. Take advantage of it. Take a long walk out to the end of the pier, and ask anybody anything you want about fishing. It's amazing how much they know and how much there is to know. They will also tell you exactly what line, bait, and hook to use and exactly where to throw it in.

The Surfside Pier tackle shop has cold drinks, crackers, and so on, but for a very good meal at a fair price, try *The Surf Diner,* right on the pier at 11 S. Ocean Blvd. The view up and down the beach and out over the Atlantic is especially nice in the mornings and evenings. The Surf is open seasonally from 6:30 a.m. to 10:30 p.m. every day. The most popular breakfast fare is their omelettes, stack of pancakes, and breakfast sandwiches. Lunch and dinners range from $6 to $20; some of the seasonal specialties are the seafood sampler basket, fresh flounder, half-pound bacon cheeseburgers, Carolina crab bisque, tuna steaks, and snow crab clusters. I also recommend saving a little room for some lemon Bundt cake or key lime pie. Call (843) 712-1850 or go to surfdiner.com.

For fishing from the beach, all you need is a rod and reel, a chair, an umbrella, and a book to read. For bait use shrimp or squid or section up a small perch. Don't forget to bring along a hollow stake to hold up the pole.

South Carolina's Riviera

Ten miles north of Surfside you'll come to the outskirts of *Myrtle Beach,* an oasis that has been called everything from the Redneck Riviera to Blue Collar Mecca to Golfer's Heaven. Each of these descriptions fits like a glove. In February and March the Canadians swarm over the place, swim in the ocean, eat the all-you-can-eat breakfasts of pancakes, eggs, and bacon, and play 18 holes in the morning and 18 more in the afternoon. Most of them drive down. So if you see four men or four women wearing golf caps with the car trunk riding low with golf clubs and the roof rack piled high with golfing paraphernalia, they're heading for Myrtle Beach and they're harmless. To celebrate their arrival, the Myrtle Beach Chamber of Commerce floods the streets with Canadian flags, street-wide Canadian banners, and Canadian everything.

Figuring each golf course down here is approximately 5.5 miles long and the South Carolina coastline has more than 100 courses, the mathematics tell us that if you laid them end to end they would extend all the way from Little River, the northernmost point in South Carolina, across all of the Georgia coastline, and more than 200 miles into Florida. In other words, there are a lot of courses down here.

Golf is just one of the attractions here. Myrtle Beach sits on the very center of the Grand Strand, a 60-mile stretch of pristine beach that is uninterrupted by tidal inlets. Much of the beach slopes gently into the water and is ideal for kids, even small ones. Campers from everywhere are welcome here; the area provides more than 12,000 campsites. The Grand Strand is also the yearly after-graduation destination for thousands of high school kids who arrive every June for a week of beach music, walking up and down the promenade, hanging out at the Pavilion, and wide-open revelry.

Finally, Myrtle Beach has become a popular retirement spot for northerners who like the weather, the beach, the golf, the food, and the general laid-back attitude. Adding all these visitors together at the height of the season, the population soars to more than 350,000. But, despite the crush and heavy commercialization, you'll find nice touches of the Old South and friendly faces everywhere.

Ten miles north of Myrtle Beach is *__Arcadian Shores Golf Club.__* This course, designed by Rees Jones, one of the premier golf architects on the scene today, combines the best of Mother Nature and the best of a modern golf course layout. The 13th and 14th holes, the signature holes, cross a cypress-studded lake that looks as if it's been here since the beginning of time. The tall pines, magnolias, and live oaks that frame the rest of the course create the perfect setting for the layout, which *Golf Magazine* and *Golf Digest* have placed in their top 50 year in and year out.

roadsigns towatchfor

On Highway 17: WELCOME TO NORTH MYRTLE BEACH, THE HOME OF VANNA WHITE

Near Andrews: WELCOME TO ANDREWS, HOME OF CHUBBY CHECKER

Guests at many area hotels are granted preferential tee times. For a weekend of top-flight golf, you'll have to go a long way to beat Arcadian Shores. For information write to Arcadian Shores Golf Club, 701 Hilton Rd., Myrtle Beach 29572; call (843) 449-5217; or check out arcadianshores.com.

Back down Highway 17 you'll see signs for ***The Dunes Golf and Beach Club.*** This is the site of the annual Golf Writers of America Clambake, which is held every year one week before the Masters. Robert Trent Jones designed the holes in such a way that the wind hits golfers from every direction on the compass. What he has done is lived up to the old Scottish saying, "No wind, no golf."

The club and clubhouse are right on the ocean, with a beautiful view of the beach. The Dunes, probably the most famous course on the beach, is a must for golfing in South Carolina. Several years ago they hosted the US Seniors Open. While the club is private, guests staying at a number of select hotels on the beach are allowed to play. So when you're making reservations, the first question you ask should not concern the rates, or if the room is on the ocean, or whether the bed comes equipped with Magic Fingers, but whether the hotel guarantees that you can play The Dunes. If it doesn't, tell them you'll call back. Then call the desk at The Dunes and ask them where you should stay. Call (843) 449-5236; write The Dunes Golf and Beach Club, 9000 N. Ocean Blvd., Myrtle Beach 29572; or visit thedunes club.net.

Both The Dunes and Arcadian Shores abound with deer and raccoons. The rare fox squirrel—bigger than a regular squirrel and with a black mask around its eyes—is sometimes seen here. Watch for it. You might also see pileated woodpeckers, alligators, and an occasional armadillo. Recently there have been several sightings of the South Florida manatee.

Years ago, the hotel and golf course owners put Myrtle Beach on the map with the introduction of the "golf package." Until then, golf resorts ran themselves like exclusive country clubs. This practice is still prevalent in most of the country, but down here the owners have gotten together to make golf not only available but affordable. As a consequence, when you check in at a hotel, you are automatically guaranteed golf course privileges on almost any of the courses in the area. Golf packages, high-quality courses, and the weather have combined to make Myrtle Beach the most popular golf destination in the world.

Cooking Fish

You scale it, clean it, load it down with cracker crumbs, and lay it gently in 550°F grease. You turn it once. Only once. The fish is done when it looks done.

On fried fish, which is the best fish, down here we eat everything—the tail, the dorsal fin, the mouth, head, eyes, and all. The cats, returning to some ancient savagery, dispose of the darker organs, then calm down to clean and polish the bones. And since any walking hound prefers fish bones to pork chop and chicken bones, the rest goes out on the step for Old Trailer and his youngest son, Boomer. In short, the cooking of fish, like of the hog and the Great Plains buffalo, is ecologically perfect; there is no waste. Fish scales are scalloped around the GOD BLESS OUR MORTGAGED HOME signs and, in the hands of an inspired artist, gilded gold and blue and magenta to liven up the seashell memorabilia that crowd the mantels from Cocoa Beach to the Outer Banks along the North Carolina coast.

BUT! There's always a but. You can't just check into any hotel and get the full golf package. So you'll have to do a little spadework to find out exactly what courses are available on your particular package.

Choosing a hotel and golf package is easier with the help of the ***Myrtle Beach Chamber of Commerce.*** Call them at (800) 356-3016, or write Myrtle Beach Area Chamber of Commerce, PO Box 2115, Myrtle Beach 29578. You can also download the *Official Myrtle Beach Area Visitors Guide,* with hotel, golf course, restaurant, and nightclub information, by visiting mbchamber.com.

Barefoot Landing, 4898 Highway 17 South, North Myrtle Beach, is a 120-shop-and-restaurant complex built on and out over the Intracoastal Waterway. The shops and restaurants here are constructed of weathered cypress-like wood and decorated with bright green awnings. Children can ride a European-style carousel, and the entire area is pleasant to stroll around and watch the ducks and the big fish in the river. Kids love this area and can be turned loose to explore. Call (800) 272-2320 or check out myrtlebeachbarefootresort.com/shopping.

A great spot to have a cold one at night on Barefoot Landing, 11 miles south of the North Carolina border, is the famous ***House of Blues*** at 4640 Highway 17 South. This is the number one spot in South Carolina for blues. The venue is housed in a Southern farmhouse–style building; the adjoining tobacco barn, appropriately enough, is the music hall site. In addition to the concerts, their restaurant features live music nightly, so no need to worry if you didn't plan ahead. The restaurant is open from 8 a.m. until 9 or 10 p.m. daily. Call (843) 272-3000 or visit houseofblues.com for a calendar of upcoming concerts.

The Pirates Voyage is a 1,000-seat theater owned by Dolly Parton. The added attraction here is you can eat a full meal while you watch the show. These shows are one of the biggest successes in the area and keep getting bigger and bigger. If you come down, be sure to catch at least one. Frankly, they are all a little bit the same. But that's all right, because the stars are all professionals and go all out to put on a good show. The theaters are high tech and state of the art. Between acts, performers sit on the edge of the stage and talk to the crowd. The prices start around $48 for adults and $24 for children. For reservations and information call (800) 433-4401 or check out piratesvoyage.com.

Myrtle Beach is the putt-putt capital of the known world. It also has a 20,000-square-foot wave pool, and for a few bucks you can take a helicopter ride around the area or parasail up and down the beach.

Ristorante Villa Romana at 707 S. King's Hwy., Myrtle Beach, is open for dinner seven days a week. A delightful place to dine, Villa Romana has strolling violinists and a gypsy accordionist. Some patrons will remember Mama Lucia, overcome by Puccini or Verdi, who danced and swayed among the tables. The specialties here are traditional Italian recipes; they serve

Music

Not only is South Carolina the birthplace of beach music and such groups as The Platters, The Coasters, and The Drifters, it's right up there at the top in blues and bluegrass. For blues, try the House of Blues at Barefoot Landing. As for bluegrass, it's best on an AM station, preferably on one of the hundred back roads that don't make the cut on most maps. If you hear the same music in a New York or Chicago traffic jam, it's just not the same. It's not even close. But when you get on some old Carolina tar-and-gravel road, with the mules and the cotton and the R.U. READY FOR ETERNITY? painted on automobile tires and nailed to the fence posts, and the dogs are all standing around in threes and fours, I guarantee it's going to make a big, big difference. Don't laugh until you try it.

More Golf Advice

Pro-Fit Inc., owned and operated by Mike Harris at 1616 Highway 17 South in North Myrtle Beach (843-361-0102), is a must stop for all serious golfers. Mike, a genuine wizard with every aspect of golf, has an amazing discovery that you must try out. For no charge he will test your clubs on a frequency vibration machine. There is a strong chance even the best and most expensive club shafts aren't matched properly. Mike will show you which ones are not in sync with the others, then he'll match them with the rest of the clubs and sell you what you need at a very moderate price. When all your clubs have the same frequency, only then are they truly matched, and only then can you swing with the same swing. While this is no guarantee to bring your handicap down, it will do wonders for your confidence, which after all is what the golf swing is all about. It works for me.

probably the best veal in the area. The soups, pasta, and bread are all made fresh daily. Prices range from $15 to $27. Call (843) 448-4990 or check out villaromanamyrtlebeach.com.

Myrtle Beach State Park, located at 4401 S. King's Hwy., is one of 47 state parks in South Carolina. Six cabins are available here (cabins 1 through 5 each sleep 6; cabin 6 sleeps 10), with rental rates ranging from $77 per night during the off season up to $200 per night for peak season; there are also weekly rates. The 350 campsites range from $24 a night for a rustic tent site to $36 a night for a full-service site in peak season. Prices are subject to change. Call (843) 238-5325 for current rates and additional information. To make reservations online, visit southcarolinaparks.reserveamerica.com.

If you would like further information on any or all of the 47 parks in the state, call *South Carolina State Parks* at (803) 734-0156. The parks are famous for their fireplace-equipped cabins, their beautiful settings, nature hikes, golf courses, and fishing expeditions. Needless to say, this is a non-profit operation, and it offers a wonderful way to visit and vacation at very reasonable prices.

Downtown in Myrtle Beach in the heart of the heart of it all is *Ripley's Believe It or Not,* at 901 N. Ocean Blvd. If you haven't been here yet, don't miss it this time. It's endless, incomprehensible, and amazing. Some of the hotter tickets at Ripley's are "Three-Ball Charlie"—the man who could put three balls in his mouth (tennis ball, golf ball, billiard ball) and whistle at the same time—a genuine Jivaro shrunken head from Ecuador, a six-legged cow, and a mock graveyard with an R.I.P. stone engraved:

Here lies an atheist,

all dressed up and

no place to go.

And who could forget "Kamala, the wolf girl, raised in the jungles of India by wolves."

Kids love this place; if you let them, they'll stay here all day. Prices are $14.99 for adults, $7.99 for kids ages 6 to 11, free for kids 5 and younger. Ripley's is open 10 a.m. to 6 p.m. Sun through Thurs, and 10 a.m. to 7 p.m. Fri and Sat. Call (843) 448-2331 or take a look at ripleys.com/myrtlebeach to see if they can make a believer out of you.

Across the street, at 916 North Blvd., is the *Gay Dolphin,* which simply defies description. You literally have to go here to believe it. Every conceivable shell design, every T-shirt, every possible item of tacky and not-so-tacky mantelpiece memorabilia, whatnot, wall hanging, and bumper sticker in the Western world is here. And the place is cavernous. My favorite bumper sticker is I don't call 911. They also carry some pretty funny postcards. One is a pitch-black card with the caption "Myrtle Beach at Midnight." Be sure to stop here. It's a standing bet, even money, that you won't leave until you buy something. Mar through Oct, hours are 9:30 a.m. to 10:30 p.m. daily except between Memorial Day and Labor Day they are open 9:30 a.m. to 11:30 p.m. Sun through Thurs, and 9:30 a.m. until midnight Fri and Sat. Nov through Feb, open daily 9 a.m. to 5:30 p.m. Call (843) 448-6550 or check out gaydolphin.com.

There are a few house rules on Myrtle Beach: Dogs must be on a leash at all times. No animals are allowed on the beach or Ocean Boulevard between 21st Avenue North and 13th Avenue South during any time of the year. No dogs are allowed on the beach between 10 a.m. and 5 p.m. from May 1 to Labor Day. Riding horses on the beach is allowed from the third Saturday in November through the end of February.

Up on the end of Highway 17 is the Little River area, which is famous for Calabash-style seafood and a wealth of brand-new and exciting golf courses. Right in the middle of Little River is *Tidewater Golf Club and*

Plantation, named in 1990 as the best new public course in the country by *Golf Magazine* and *Golf Digest.* Once again, this is a public course open to almost anyone with a set of sticks. All you have to do is call (843) 913-2424 for a tee time and bring plenty of balls for the water holes.

The great secret of Tidewater's unique success lies with Ken Tomlinson, the course designer. He has laid out multiple landing areas for each tee, a design feature that allows players of every level to play the same iron from fairway to green on each hole. Another of Ken's wise decisions here at Tidewater is that he has given the course the best land possible—the high, wooded peninsula that lies between the Atlantic Ocean and the Intracoastal Waterway. And still another feature of the course is that Ken doesn't believe in the dreary 90-degree use of carts on the fairways. On most days you can drive them right down the middle and save yourself a lot of club carrying and unnecessary walking. Ken says, "Hell, it's only grass." This is a superb course and it stays in beautiful shape. For further information write Tidewater Golf Club and Plantation, 1400 Tidewater Dr., North Myrtle Beach 29582. You can investigate their golf packages and book tee times at tidewatergolf.com.

On Highway 501 past Conway and Aynor, you'll come to the town of *Galivants Ferry.* Right here is the center for the longest-running political gathering in the country, the *Galivants Ferry Stump,* which occurs here every May. It is organized by the Holliday family, who also oversee the largest tobacco farm in operation in South Carolina as well as a number of diverse business interests throughout Horry County. In 1979 the Hollidays were honored for their contribution to the economic progress of the area and for their public service to South Carolina by the Department of Highways and Public Transportation, which renamed the section of US 501 between Galivants Ferry and Conway the Holliday Highway.

John Holliday, his brother Joseph, and their families have been personally responsible for continuing a tradition their grandfather began in 1876—the Galivants Ferry Democratic Stump Speaking. John Holliday says, "I remember sitting on a wagon in a thicket, drinking cherry cola while 50 to 75 people stood on a stump or some boards to speak. The Stump started when there was only a Democratic party in the state. We didn't even know how to spell Republican."

John and his brother Joseph have continued another tradition started by their grandfather: Each of them has been the postmaster of Galivants Ferry.

A stop here at the general store right on the highway and a chance to meet one of the family, who will tell you all about the place and certainly invite you to the May meeting, is definitely a once-in-a-lifetime experience.

The *Original Benjamin's Calabash Seafood and Nautical Museum,* located at 9593 N. Kings Hwy., Myrtle Beach, is a one-of-a-kind masterpiece. It offers a 170-item buffet with crab legs and country food, a carving station, a pasta station, and seafood, soup, salad, and dessert bars. It can seat and serve over 500 guests at a time. As you first enter the restaurant, you will see the world's largest model of the *Queen Elizabeth,* the actual one that was shown to the queen before the ship was built in her honor. Next you will see the dry sea aquarium, which houses the largest collection of mounted fish in the Southeast. As advertised, all the fish were alive at one time. You will also see the largest replica of the *Mayflower.* The rest of the lobby and the many rooms that make up Benjamin's Original Calabash are filled with compasses, telescopes, underwater cameras, buoys, anchors, aquariums, and much, much more. There is also a full-size shark hanging outside the front door. In other words, Benjamin's Calabash Restaurant has to be seen to be believed. And the food and service is probably the best on the beach.

Beware, this is the original *Benjamin's Calabash.* There are other Calabashes along the beach, and a few are even using the names Ben and Benjamin's. But in the words of the circus, "Be not deceived by envious competitors." All you have to do is try Original Benjamin's and you will stray no farther. Open daily from 2:30 p.m. to whenever dinner is over. Call (800) 288-8687 for group reservations. For further information visit Benjamin's at originalbenjamins.com.

Another fine inn on the beach is *The Islander Inn* at 57 W. 1st St., Ocean Isle Beach, North Carolina, offering the very finest lodging, accommodations, and expert assistance for the golf enthusiast. Highly recommended are the Pearl Courses (East and West). I've played both, and they are outstanding. The inn features an indoor heated pool and an outdoor oceanfront pool with a sun deck. In case you think you're too far north of South Carolina, keep in mind you're only 10 miles from Little River. Call them at (888) 325-4753 or visit islanderinn.com.

Stop at *125 Oyster Bar and Grill* at 125 Causeway Dr., Ocean Isle Beach, for fresh local seafood served fried, blackened, grilled, or broiled. Steaks, burgers, and sandwiches round out the dinner fare starting at 5 p.m.

They also offer a daily breakfast bar served from 7:30 to 11 a.m. This casual neighborhood watering hole comes complete with dart boards, pool table, and 11—count 'em, 11—TV screens. A great spot to relax, eat, and watch your favorite game. Live entertainment on weekends. Open daily; call (910) 575-7500 for more information.

The Museum of Coastal Carolina, the area's premier museum of natural history, is located at 21 E. 2nd St., Ocean Isle Beach. It is an ideal place to bring the family, especially the kids. Family programs about nature include guided beach, marsh, and bird walks. Topics cover snakes, alligators, fossils, shells, birds of prey, fish and fishing, and Native American lore. For small children, there is a hands-on-activity area, complete with bones, shells, skulls, hides, and magnification devices. In addition there is a Touch Tank Feeding for feeding small sea creatures every Fri at 11 a.m. Open Thurs through Sat 10 a.m. to 4 p.m. Admission is $9 for adults, $6 for students, and $4 for children ages 3 and 4. Call (910) 579-1016 or visit their website at museumofcc.org.

Ten miles north of Ocean Isle, go to Southport and pick up the ferry to one of the most amazing and most beautiful islands in the Atlantic—***Bald Head Island,*** North Carolina. Departing from Indigo Plantation on W. 9th Street in Southport (910-457-5003), you will head out to the island, go on

A Sample of North Carolina

Let's face it, Myrtle Beach is getting crowded. So is North Myrtle Beach. If you want to play golf, stay at a great place, be on the ocean, and get away from the traffic and bustle, all you have to do is drive 8 to 10 miles north of Tidewater Golf Club and Plantation in Little River (see description earlier in this section). You can cross the North Carolina line without a passport. And the natives are friendly.

A great spot to stop and look around would be **Ocean Isle Beach** and the **Ocean Isle Inn,** at 37 W. 1st St. Call (800) 352-5988 or (910) 579-0750; ocean isleinn.com. From here you are within 10 minutes of 36 championship golf courses in North and South Carolina and some of the finest food and fishing in the world. Unlike most East Coast beaches, which run north–south, Ocean Island is east–west oriented, which lets you see some of the most incredible sunrises and sunsets imaginable. This is the perfect place for family vacations, reunions, club outings, or romantic getaways.

the tour, have lunch, and return. The round-trip fee is $24.75 per adult and $13.75 per child age 3 to 12. While out on Bald Head, you can look over the very fine golf course and the accommodations, see the famous Old Baldy Lighthouse, and decide when you want to come back to spend a few days. Most of this remarkable island has been given over to the state wildlife commission and is now a bird and turtle sanctuary. It also has one of the finest stands of live oaks and maritime forests on the coast. Pelicans and giant herons are everywhere, and at night there is a good chance you will see a loggerhead. Another bonus is that there are no cars except maintenance vehicles.

If you are going to do one thing and one thing only in North Carolina, here's what you do: Go to Bald Head, and play 18 holes on the truly great course lined with live oaks, herons, egrets, pelicans, and almost any kind of wildlife you can imagine. Then have a cool one at the bar overlooking the rocks and surf while you watch the sun slowly set, and luxuriously reflect on what a great day it has been and how you might just very well stay. A good place to start looking for information is baldheadislandinformation.com.

Nearby at Highway 301 and I-95 in Hamer is **South of the Border** (or SOB, as it's known to insiders), an amalgam of South Carolina and Old Mexico—a yellow and pink Tijuana backed in black velvet. Pedro, a 97-foot statue, straddles the entrance and is billed as "the largest freestanding sign east of the Mississippi." You can drive in between his legs. Inside they have the biggest, brightest, tackiest assortment of what is affectionately called memorabilia, which runs the gamut from 8 types of back-scratchers to at least 30, and still counting, types of coffee mugs. They also have flags of every description, clever bumper stickers, tapes, CDs, and woodcuts of GOD BLESS OUR MORTGAGED HOME. South Carolinians claim they wouldn't be caught dead here, but the place is packed, and if you want a room, you'll have to call in advance for a reservation. Call (800) 845-6011. Visit their website at thesouthoftheborder.com, but don't expect it to be "politically correct."

Places to Stay in the Grand Strand

GEORGETOWN

Mansfield Plantation
1776 Mansfield Rd.
(866) 717-1776
mansfieldplantation.com

Shaw House
613 Cypress Ct.
(843) 546-9663
bbonline.com/sc/
shawhouse

MYRTLE BEACH

Serendipity Inn
407 71st Ave. North
(800) 762-3229
serendipityinn.com

PAWLEYS ISLAND

Litchfield Plantation
24 Avenue of Live Oaks
(843) 543-3146
litchfieldplantation.net

Places to Eat in the Grand Strand

MURRELLS INLET

Lee's Inlet Kitchen
4460 Highway 17
Business
(843) 651-2881
leesinletkitchen.com

Nance's Creek Front Restaurant
4883 Highway 17
Business
(843) 651-2696
nancescreekfront
restaurant.com

Salt Water Creek
4660 Highway 17 Bypass
(843) 357-2433
saltwatercreek.com

PAWLEYS ISLAND

Frank's Restaurant & Bar
10434 Ocean Hwy.
(843) 237-3030
franksandoutback.com

SURFSIDE BEACH

The Surf Diner
11 S. Ocean Blvd.
(843) 712-1850
surfdiner.com

Tobacco & Cotton Lands

You might want to get your compass out to picture the geography here. South Carolina is roughly a triangle covering 30,000 square miles, 500 of which are inland lakes. From the northwest corner, near the Chattooga River, a rough and jagged line runs east for 330 miles to Little River Inlet, marking the boundary between South and North Carolina. To the west, the Savannah River extends southeast from that same northwest corner for 240 miles to Tybee Sound, which separates the state from Georgia and lies adjacent to Savannah. And on the east coast, the Atlantic shoreline stretches roughly 200 miles between Little River and Tybee Sound. The state is drained by three main river systems: the Pee Dee in the northeast, the Santee in the central area, and the Savannah in the southeast. The swift flow of the rivers in the Upcountry has led most of the state's manufacturing plants to select sites in that section. Below the Fall Line—which runs across the state and separates the Up from the Low—these red, mud-laden rivers become wide and clear, depositing their silt on the bottom. Stained black with tannic acid from cypress and other roots, the rivers run slowly under the live oaks and tupelos through the flat, rich soils to the Atlantic Ocean.

The area in the northeast around the muddy Pee Dee River is called the Pee Dee section, and right in the middle of it is the city of **Florence.** The city is in the heart of the tobacco region of the state. A visit to Florence, which is 65 miles from the coast, is interesting in that it shows how an old downtown section of a small town can still compete with a brand-new sprawling mall a few miles away.

Florence has been nicknamed "Tooth City," "Tooth Capital," and "Denture Capital of the World" due to the reputation of the **Sexton Dental Clinic,** at 377 W. Palmetto St. It advertises "affordable general dentistry," so people come from as far away as Hawaii and Alaska because of the low prices and the fact that work is done by the assembly-line method and almost anything, even full dentures top and bottom, can be done right here in one day. They're open Mon through Fri from 6 a.m. to 5 p.m., and they accept major credit cards. Call (843) 662-2543. Their website is sexton dental.net.

At lunchtime, head to **Red Bone Alley** at 1903 W. Palmetto St. This is an amazing combination restaurant, bar, sports bar, and game room. The ceiling is at least 30 feet high, and you are surrounded by sides of houses depicting the various styles of architecture that characterize Charleston, Williamsburg, San Francisco, and so on. They serve a very good lunch here for $10; dinners are around $17. The full menu is at redbonealley .com. The game room features a CD jukebox with more than 1,000 selections. Three pool tables and an air hockey setup are also here. One of the pool tables is L-shaped with eight pockets. Weird. You must be over 21 to use the game room, or be accompanied by an adult or parent. Call (843) 673-0035.

After lunch, be sure to stop by the **Florence Museum,** if for no other reason than to see the extraordinary work of William Henry Johnson, who painted here in 1940. His childlike but incredibly moving painting *Evening* was painted on rough burlap; his *Christmas Party* and *Rooftops of Denmark* are also worth a peek. Picasso once said it took him 20 years to learn to paint like Rembrandt but all his life to learn to paint like a child. Picasso would have loved Johnson's work. The museum is located at 558 Spruce St. Open Tues through Sat 10 a.m. to 5 p.m. and Sun 2 to 5 p.m. Admission

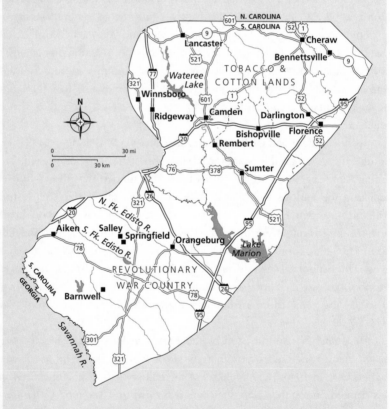

is free and donations are welcomed. Call (843) 662-3351 or check out their calendar of events at florencemuseum.org.

Northeast of Florence, 15 miles away, is **Darlington,** founded in 1785 and the home of the **Bojangles' Southern 500,** which is held every May. The **Darlington Raceway** at 1301 Harry Byrd Pkwy., on Highway 52, is so big and commanding, there is no way to miss it. Inside the main gate is an interesting museum that features 15 old racing cars, each equipped with an audio module that tells the history of the car, where and when it ran, and who drove it. Also available is every conceivable piece of memorabilia you can think of, from jackets and caps to postcards and testimonials from famous drivers. Admission is $5 for adults; children under 12 are admitted free. Open Mon through Fri from 10 a.m. to 5 p.m., Sat 10 a.m. to 4 p.m., and Sun 11 a.m. to 4 p.m. Call (843) 395-8821.

For those who would just like to see the track, walk down to the white security building at the end of the fence that runs along the front. The guard there will give you permission to climb up the short walk, where you can

TOP RECOMMENDATIONS IN THE FALL LINE

The Chitlin Strut
Salley
(803) 258-3485
chitlinstrut.com

Darlington Raceway
1301 Harry Byrd Pkwy.
Darlington
(843) 395-8900
darlingtonraceway.com

Florence Museum
558 Spruce St.
Florence
(843) 662-3351
florencemuseum.org

Palmetto Golf Club
275 Berrie Rd. Southwest
Aiken
(803) 649-2951
palmettogolfclub.net

Springfield Frog Jump
Springfield
(803) 258-3152

Swan Lake Iris Gardens
Sumter
(803) 436-2500
irisfestival.org

Willcox Inn
100 Colleton Ave.
Aiken
(800) 434-6835
thewillcox.com

see the great expanse of curving concrete that is the track. You can also see the stands and the giant billboards. It's a sight you won't soon forget. You can get the latest NASCAR news at darlingtonraceway.com.

In the center of the town is a giant mural 100 feet long and 20 feet high painted by Blue Sky, a Columbian artist whose work can be found all over the state. The mural is a rendering of how the old city looked at the turn of the century when a huge oak was the centerpiece of the old town square.

Lee State Park is only 7 miles away on the banks of the Lynches River at 487 Loop Rd., Bishopville. The park is open all year and is especially suited for horseback riding. Although they don't provide horses, they do have a stable, a very fine bridle path, and a show ring. Walking-around admission is free; campsites are $15 to $18 per night. Call (800) 345-5307. There's more information at southcarolinaparks.com/lee. It was here in 1880 that the last duel in the state was fought. The contestants were Colonel William S. Shannon of Camden and Colonel E. B. C. Cash of Cheraw. They met at Dubose's Bridge, which was in neutral territory. Colonel Shannon was mortally wounded, and his death resulted in a state law against dueling. Up until 1954, South Carolina public officials had to swear they had not engaged in a duel since January 1, 1881, and that they would not engage in dueling during their term of office.

An even more flamboyant episode in Pee Dee country history was the "Darlington War" of 1894. This was an outbreak caused by Governor B. R. "Pitchfork Ben" Tillman's liquor regulations, particularly his order permitting private homes to be searched without warrant for concealed liquor. In the first skirmish two citizens and one constable were killed, and a number of others were injured. A day later Darlingtonians fired on a train bringing in more constables and began scouring the countryside for other lawmen. Tillman countered by bringing in the militia, but many companies refused to obey and were dishonorably discharged. Among these was the Charleston company, whose members declined to surrender their arms and went on to defend their action in federal court against "one B. R. Tillman, styling himself Governor of South Carolina." Tillman finally collected more docile troops, but by this time the Darlington Guards, a local vigilante group, had restored the peace.

The *Darlington County Historical Commission* is housed in the old city jail at 204 Hewitt St. Inside are wonderful photographs from more than

100 years ago that portray the history of the town, the growth and decline of the cotton empire, the introduction of the automobile, and other notable events and facts. Also on exhibit are a copy of Stephen Foster's original lyrics for "Way Down upon the Swanee River." Originally the river was the Pee Dee, which runs nearby, and you can see where he scratched it out on the manuscript and changed it to Swanee. No one seems to know why. Hours are 9 a.m. to 5 p.m. Mon through Fri. No admission charge. Phone (843) 398-4710. There's more at darcosc.com/historicalcommission.

Outside Bishopville on I-20 heading west, you'll come to a series of cotton and soybean fields that are as flat as a parking lot. Right in the middle, at Charlene's Lane, is a big, 6-foot-high red neon sign spelling out simply EAT. It's one of those signs you wonder about. Well, pull off and stop by here. The food is down-home Southern and very good. The new name is **Charlene's Taste of Country,** and they specialize in fried chicken, country-fried steak, great fresh vegetables, and lush desserts. Prices are low, from $6 to $9. No kidding. Charlene made *Southern Living*'s "Favorite Regional Restaurant" list. That says a great deal. Call (803) 428-2900.

But before you leave Bishopville, you need to stop by **Pearl Fryar's place.** If you haven't heard of Pearl (that's the name his mama gave him), you should have, because he is one fine gardener extraordinaire. It all started when he took home a couple of castaway plants from a nearby nursery and started practicing a technique called topiary pruning. Well, one thing led to another, and the next thing he knew, his 3-acre yard became a showplace for his creativity and skill. There are topiary animals, abstract geometric shapes, and even traditional quatrefoils, some reaching high into the sky. On my last visit I pulled over just in front of a large bus, which deposited 50 or so admiring visitors. We all felt as if we had just stepped out into a fantasy land. Admission is free, but donations are accepted at a simple box on-site. With any luck you just might find Pearl tending his garden, where he is happy to share his creations with you. His address is 165 Broad Acres Rd., and the garden is open Tues through Sat from 10 a.m. to 4 p.m. year-round. See pearlfryar.com for directions. You'll know you're getting close when you pass the Waffle House with the topiary out front. You guessed it—Pearl created and maintains it, and his breakfast is on the house.

One of the older and prouder Fall Line towns is **Winnsboro,** the seat of Fairfield County. It was settled in 1755 and named for Colonel Richard Winn,

Revolutionary officer and early town father. Pennsylvanians, Virginians, and North Carolinians settled here, but along with them came many from the Low Country who were seeking a more healthful climate and broader cotton lands.

roadsidesigns

Near Winnsboro a grocery store sign reads simply DE STO.

Thirty years ago at the corner of Congress and Washington stood a Confederate monument of a lone soldier facing north. After a few of the local "tosspots" banged their Fords and Chevys into it and tried to climb it, it was moved to the park two blocks away. Needless to say, the city fathers saw to it that the soldier still faces north.

The centerpiece of this old town, along with its Confederate soldier, is the town clock and belfry at the corner of Washington and Main. The bell was used as an alarm for fires and curfews and to let the villagers know that fresh meat was available. Legend has it that there were beaten paths from every direction made by dogs who knew the sound of the bell meant fresh meat for them as well as their masters.

The bell for the clock was made in France, and the story goes that for a long time it had a clear and silvery tone. In 1895, during a fire, it was rung so vigorously that it cracked and had to be sent to Philadelphia for repairs. When it was finally returned, the old-timers reported it had lost its silvery tone, and it was doubtful whether or not it was the original bell. In spite of the cracked bell and the shoddy northern repairs, the old clock is the longest continuously running town clock in the United States.

Heading east on Highway 34, you'll be through the community of Rockton before you realize it. As a matter of fact, the railroad crossing is the community. On the immediate right you'll see an outdoor museum with no one in attendance. It's the **South Carolina Railroad Museum.** If you're a railroad buff, you can stop and look over the old steam engines and cabooses; they even have a 1930 day coach. Every year a new train or caboose or old engine is added to the collection. And every fall an old-fashioned steam engine cranks up and pulls a few day coach cars up into the mountains for a look at the changing of the leaves. It's a fascinating trip. To learn more about this trip and their other scheduled runs, visit scrm.org.

Roadside Serenade

In small towns there is no law against dogs running loose, and every night you'll see three, four, and five gathering under the streetlights and planning their evening. When we lived in Winnsboro, right up the road from Columbia, nine of them wound up living on our porch. I, like a fool, not only bought them food but paid their vet bills and bought them couches and overstuffed chairs from the Salvation Army. One was named Zeke, a direct descendant of one of the somersaulting terriers from the Hunt Brothers Circus, which used to have their winter quarters up the road in Gaffney. At night all nine would line up in full chorus when the trains went through at 2 and 4 in the morning, and it was the most god-awful beautiful sound I will ever hear.

On Highway 34 coming into the town of Ridgeway, you might want to stop at **The Thomas Company** at 105 N. Palmer St. This is a combination gift shop, coffee shop and deli, and tearoom all in one place. Downstairs the gift shop has a nice assortment of items such as handcrafted quilts, teapots, jewelry, soaps, and gourmet foods perfect for assembling a gift basket. The Coffee Shop Deli offers a community table for visiting with locals while enjoying a latte or smoothie and deli sandwich. Or, if you prefer, you can choose your own table for a quiet lunch. Laura's Tea Room upstairs is a charming place to savor one of their fragrant teas with a scone, soup, or quiche. The ladies will love this one. Cream Tea is served from 10:30 a.m. to 2 p.m. Tues through Fri, and High Tea is 11 a.m. to 2 p.m. Tues through Sat and Sun by reservation only. The Coffee Shop Deli is open Mon through Sat from 10:30 a.m. to 3 p.m., and Sun 12:30 to 4 p.m. The gift shop stays open from 9 a.m. to 5 p.m. Tues through Sat and 12:30 to 4 p.m. Sun. Reservations are strongly recommended for Laura's Tea Room. Call (803) 337-8594 or visit laurastearoom.com.

Another fun stop is the **Ruff and Company Mercantile** on Highway 21 (165 Palmer St.), a general store kind of place that has been in business since 1840. In fact, it's run by the sixth generation of the Ruff family, who operate it and the "new" store just next door, which was added in 1901. The inventory is just about the same as it has always been—a wide variety of hard-to-find items and general necessities. Here and at their furniture store across the street, you'll see everything from outdoor rockers and porch swings to mattresses and children's toys. This is a real step back in time to the midlands of our grandparents' heyday.

Be sure to take the three-block walking tour of *Ridgeway* and its antebellum and Victorian houses. There is the beautiful Victorian *Robert Charleton Thomas House,* 120 Dogwood Ave., constructed in 1906. Note the mounting block in the corner of the front yard. This large block of granite allowed young ladies to step delicately into their awaiting carriages.

The *Augustus Talley Moore House* was built in 1899. Mr. Moore's young son was so distressed at seeing a local crippled man that he swore to repair the foot one day. A. T. Moore grew up to become a fine doctor, and he perfected and patented the first artificial hip socket. The first surgery he performed was to repair the foot of the crippled man he had seen as a child.

The *Charles Wray House* on Peach Street at the corner of Highway 34 is an enormous and imposing home. Residents say if you look carefully at the attic windows, you may see Charles Wray, who built this home in 1910, staring down the railroad tracks in search of his wife and child, who were killed with him in a tragic train accident.

Revolutionary War Country

Highway 34 east takes you back into *Camden.* Established in 1732, it is the oldest inland town in the state. For nearly a century Camden was noted for its duels and was the mecca for gentlemen seeking instruction in the code of honor, but this era came to a close in 1880 when dueling was outlawed after the Cash-Shannon duel in Darlington. In 1791, at the corner of Bull and Broad Streets, George Washington addressed the local citizens, but what he said has been lost in the mists of history.

The approach to the town is over the Wateree River Bridge and then through a half-mile of luxurious magnolia trees that seem to stay in bloom all spring and summer. Camden is the home of *The Carolina Cup Steeplechase* in April and *The Colonial Cup Steeplechase* in November. If you're here during these times, you can watch the natives drinking champagne as they motor out to the track in their antique cars. Arriving here, they will often spread out an enormous Oriental rug and, after securing the corners with huge vases of cut flowers, arrange a fine silver and crystal picnic in the middle of the infield. Once in a while a group will outdo all the others by showing up in elaborate evening clothes accompanied by a string quartet and, I'm not kidding, a chandelier. If you're interested in attending this event, call (803) 432-6513 or visit carolina-cup.org.

The **Historic Camden Revolutionary War Site,** located at 222 Broad St., is a 107-acre outdoor museum complex open seven days a week, except major holidays. This is the site of the original town of Camden, which was fortified by the British in 1780. Portions of the palisade walls have been rebuilt where they originally stood. The old mansion, built on the war site by Joseph Kershaw, one of the town fathers, was used as British headquarters during the occupation. It has been reconstructed and can be seen on any of the walking tours of the area. There's more at historic-camden.net.

For a walking tour of Camden, call the **Kershaw County Chamber of Commerce & Visitors Center** at (803) 432-2525. A quicker, more romantic tour in a horse-drawn carriage can be very colorful. For information, write to the **Camden Carriage Company,** PO Box 1082, Camden 29020, or call

The Patriot and South Carolina

It wasn't until I saw Mel Gibson in *The Patriot*—an excellent movie that should be required viewing for every South Carolina native—and reread my history that I discovered South Carolina had 245 skirmishes and battles during the Revolutionary War. In fact, most of the war was fought right here. Some of this truly beautiful movie was shot down in the swamps and plantations of the Low Country around Charleston and Beaufort, but most of it was filmed upstate, where much of the war took place.

If you're interested in history, the Camden-Winnsboro area 30 miles north of Columbia would be the ideal place to trace most of the action and events. As a matter of fact, at the Historic Camden Revolutionary War Site, located 1.4 miles from I-20 on the outskirts of Camden, they offer guided interactive tours, complete with a videotape made by SC ETV about the Battle of Camden. Only a mile away you can visit the Baron DeKalb Memorial, designed by Robert Mills, who also designed the Washington Monument. DeKalb was the German-born French citizen who became a general in the Continental Army and was mortally wounded during the Battle of Camden. He is buried at a downtown church. The two major battles fought here—the Battle of Camden and the Battle of Hobkirk Hill—resulted in British General Cornwallis's retreat north and his eventual surrender to Washington at Yorktown, Virginia, in October 1781.

them at (803) 425-5737. Most of the 60-odd houses seen on either the walking tour or the carriage tour are private homes and may only be viewed from the street. A few, however, are available for interior tours. Check with the Kershaw County Chamber of Commerce for this information.

For an excellent bed-and-breakfast in downtown Camden, **The Bloomsbury Inn,** located at 1707 Lyttleton St., is at the head of the list. Dating back to 1849, the house is steeped in history and is rated one of the top 10 bed-and-breakfasts in the United States. This is the home where Mary Boykin Chesnut wrote her famous *Diary from Dixie*. Room rates range from $149 to $215 per night. Call (803) 432-5858 or visit bloomsburyinn.com to make your reservation.

In September 1989 Hurricane Hugo hit not only the Carolina coast but, to everyone's surprise, came barreling inland with winds of more than 110 miles an hour through Sumter, Camden, and all the way up to Charlotte. Camden's big trailer park a few miles to the south of the center of town was devastated; most of the units were completely destroyed. The damage has been repaired, but every September and October people around here begin checking the weather reports and keeping a wary eye on the sky. A calypso song from the Low Country by way of Barbados tells us the months to watch.

June too soon
July stand by
August almost
September remember
October not over

You might need some sustenance after a walking or carriage tour, so head to the **Old Armory Steakhouse** at 514 Rutledge St. (803-432-3222). Although Camden is 100 miles from the coast, the seafood selection here is varied, ample, and served broiled or fried. The Old Armory Signature Steak, a hand-cut 12-ounce New York strip seared with cracked peppercorns, is especially good and comes with Tabasco onion straws and jumbo fried shrimp. All of the steaks come with your choice of either their Gorgonzola or portobello port wine reduction sauce. Dinner prices run from around $10 for popcorn shrimp to about $26 for the 9-ounce filet mignon. For lunch they have $6 specials like their chicken salad croissant or fried flounder sandwich. The Old Armory's hours are Mon and Tues 11 a.m. to 9 p.m. and Wed through Sat 11 a.m. to 10 p.m. See oldarmorysteakhouse.com for the complete menu.

One of the best reasons for visiting Camden is to get your bearings and be able to find the town of **Boykin** about 20 miles away. Take Highway 521 south and turn right at Highway 261. Drive 4 miles or so and there you are—that is, if you haven't missed it. It's on the left side of the road, and you have to watch for it.

The millpond and other properties here are owned by the heirs of Lemuel Whitaker Boykin II, six generations from the original 1775 settler, William Boykin II. The entire community, which consists of the Boykin Company Grille and Store, the Broom Place, the Swift Creek Baptist Church, the Mill Pond Steakhouse, and the Boykin Mill, is listed on the National Register of Historic Places. Groups are welcome and tours are available.

At the **Boykin Company Grille and Store,** 81 Boykin Mill Rd., Rembert, you can get breakfast or a light lunch and then sit out on the porch and watch the road. Almost nothing comes along but an occasional slow-moving dog or an even slower-moving buzzard. The store, with wooden shelves to the high ceiling, sells, among other goods, Boykin's Unsalted Water Ground Grits, stick candy, and raspberry, wild blackberry, and buttered maple syrups. You can even catch some bluegrass sounds around dinnertime on weekends.

Any of the Boykins that are around will be glad to take you on a tour of the 100-year-old mill a few yards away. You'll see grits and meal ground the way they've been ground down here, by water power on hand-dressed millstones, for more than 200 years. Cornmeal, for the record, is finely ground grits. When you see and feel the oil in the fresh grits made here, you'll realize that what you haul down from the supermarket shelves is not only a sin but a true tragedy. The general store is open 9 a.m. to 6 p.m. Call (803) 432-0076.

Located at 84 Boykin Mill Rd., the **Mill Pond Steakhouse,** one of the very best restaurants in the state, is made up of three buildings, all on the National Register of Historic Places. The building on the left is an elaborate kitchen; the one in the middle is a small dining room with an old-fashioned marble fountain counter serving as a bar; and the one on the right is the main dining room, overlooking the very picturesque millpond, which feeds the mill a couple hundred feet away.

A quick glance at the comments left by guests in the guest book will give you a rough idea of the quality of the food here. From Columbia we hear, "First time—no doggie bag." From Charleston, "Slow but good." From Greenville, "Hard as hell to find but worth it." From Chester, "Ya'll need sweet tea." And finally from Darlington, "Yeeeee-haw!" It's even better than that. Open for dinner from 5 to 10 p.m. (at 2 p.m. for lighter fare) Tues through Sat. Call (803) 425-8825 for reservations, which I recommend highly. Take a look at boykinmillfarms.com for more on all the properties.

Quail hunters of the world should know that Boykin is the home of the Boykin spaniel. Right here is where the Boykin family bred the dog, trained it, and introduced it to the hunting world. For further information on this, you can call the **Boykin Spaniel Society** at (803) 425-1032. Their website is loaded with information at boykinspaniel.org.

South Carolina not only leads the nation in poisonous snakes—we have seven kinds—it's also up there on the top 10 list of fast-food stores per square mile. If you stay on the main roads, you'll see them lined up cheek-by-jowl, and if you're downwind, the grease is so thick you'll have to use your wipers. So stay on the back roads as much as possible—back where they paint ARE YOU READY FOR JESUS? on the rocks and the automobile tires swing in the chinaberry trees.

Highway 261 out of Boykin, heading back toward Camden, is a back road. Turn right at Highway 521 toward Sumter, and 10 or so miles down the road is Rembert, the home of **Lilfred's,** one of the very best European restaurants in the Carolinas and Georgia, located at 8425 Camden Hwy. When you're this far off the beaten path, you have to be good to attract the crowd they have been attracting for the past 40-odd years. People come here from everywhere. And they keep coming back. Some of Lilfred's specialties are New York strip steak, free-range chicken, oysters on the half shell, and onion rings, but the menu may change due to seasonal selections. Prices are $15 to $35 for dinner. It's worth it. Open 5:30 to 9:30 p.m. Thurs through Sat. Check them out at lilfreds.net, or call (803) 432-8750.

South of Rembert on Highway 521, you'll come to the home of **Shaw Air Force Base** on Highway 378. Many of the attack planes that were used in Desert Storm and Iraqi Freedom came from here. When you drive by, you can see them out on the ramps, shooting landings and takeoffs. This restricted base is usually not open to the public, but with advance notice (two weeks minimum) tours can be arranged for groups of 15 or more. Children must be 12 or older. For more information call (803) 895-2019. The official website is shaw.af.mil.

Ward's Barbecue, 416 E. Liberty St., Sumter (803-775-2490), is open only on Thurs, Fri, and Sat from 10:30 a.m. to 7:30 p.m. They are closed Sun, Mon, and Tues, and cooking is done on Wed. Eating barbecue down here is usually done on the weekends, so most barbecue places follow this schedule. At Ward's you can have a barbecue sandwich with coleslaw for $3.65. Soft drinks are available in the vending machine outside. You sit outside on cement chairs at a cement table and watch the trains go by. If you like corn dodgers, which are the same as hush puppies, they are available at $2 per dozen. For you barbecue experts out there, Ward's was written up a while back on roadfood.com. Be advised, their sauce is ketchup-based. They also have three other Sumter locations.

At the other end of Liberty Street is *Swan Lake Iris Gardens,* one of the most attractive and best-run free city parks in the state. One-hundred-foot-high longleaf pine and cypress trees surround the 50-acre lake. Be sure to take a long look at the cypress knees sticking up from the water—this is how the tree breathes. Out on the lake are eight different kinds of swans

Bombing & Strafing

Here's a slam-dunk winner that you will never, ever forget. Shaw Field (Air Force Base), located 30 miles east of Columbia on Highway 378, has provided a state-of-the-art showcase like nothing in the entire country. Out on the Poinsett Electronic Combat Range, which features combat planes practicing low-altitude bombing and very low-altitude strafing runs, Shaw Field personnel have erected a set of bleachers for the curious. It's a huge mound with bleachers on top. If you look to the left, you will see the bombing; to the right, the strafing—only 200 yards from where you're sitting. You will also see many of the high-speed planes that fought in Desert Storm and more recent conflicts in Iraq and Afghanistan. Bring your cameras and earplugs. This is a real experience, and your kids will love you forever. Normally open from 8 a.m. to sunset Mon through Thurs and 8 a.m. to 1 p.m. on Fri (except for the third Fri each month). Since the schedule varies from week to week, call (803) 895-2597 for exact times.

from all over the world, along with ducks, geese, and herons. May is the big season for the **Iris Festival** (irisfestival.org). This is when the six million Japanese irises planted here come into bloom. Azaleas, camellias, and roses also bloom in profusion. An old fire engine is available for kids to climb on, under, and over, which they do by the hour. Visit sumtersc.gov or call (803) 436-2500 for more information on this beautiful park.

Due south of Sumter on Highway 6 is **Santee State Park.** This immense tract of land is devoted to fishing, camping, hiking, biking, and tennis on the shores of Lake Marion, one of the biggest lakes in the state. Once again, since this is a nonprofit state park, the prices for lodging, golf, camping, fishing, and so on are very reasonable. For information write Santee State Park, 251 State Park Rd., Santee 29142; call (803) 854-2408; or visit southcarolinaparks.com/santee.

Due west of Santee on Highway 301 and then on Highway 4, you'll come to the old railroad town of Springfield, where the tracks run right down Main Street. **The Springfield Frog Jump** is the main event here and is held in April every year. Call (803) 258-3152 for exact dates and information. The owner of the winner of the event and the frog itself—you can raise your own frog, or you can buy one from the local kids—are flown out to Calaveras County, California, for the National Jump-Off. The contest here is staged in the middle of the town. After considerable music and ballyhoo about the history and significance of the frog jump, the contestants are asked to step up on the platform and announce where they are from, to whom they are related, and what their frog's name is. Following this the dignitaries lead the contestants and their frogs out to the launching pad. Old-timers in their 90s and children barely out of their mother's arms can and do enter the contest. The frogs' names run the gamut from Flash to Captain Marvel to Spiro Agnew to Desert Storm.

The method of operation is simple: The frog takes three jumps and the overall length is measured. One enterprising contestant with his eye on the California jump-off introduced his frog to a nonlethal snake at the last second before launching, hoping to scare it into a greater jump. This proved disastrous. The frog froze, relieved himself, and had to be taken away, still staring out into the middle distance; it recovered later and jumped in the consolation trials. The Carolina record is an 18-foot jump, but for the past 20 years most of the Calaveras County, California, winners have been from the West Coast.

Healing Springs

If you have given up on the medical profession and over-the-counter med
and are suffering from backaches, legaches, and head-, shoulder-, and fo
aches, there is still hope. It's not only cheap, it's free. All you have to do is get
there. And the trip is very, very pleasant. From Columbia take SC 302 south to
US 178 and turn left. Continue on 178 until you hit SC 3. Turn right on Healing
Springs Road, which is clearly marked. Turn right again on Healing Springs Court.
If you see cows in a field, you've gone too far. Back up until you see the stream
and 12 spouts that never stop running. This is it!

The hard fact is that every month, thousands of people venture down these very
same roads to Healing Springs to wash and drink and carry home the magical
elixir. Some carry as many as 100 one-gallon milk jugs filled with it. A test conducted years ago revealed that city or county water will turn green and slimy in
a jar after a few months, but the water from Healing Springs will remain clear.
Legend has it that the Cherokee Indians first discovered it and used it until one
Nathanial Walker purchased it from a tribal chief for a few bags of grain. Since
then the property has gone through six owners until 1944, when the late L. P.
Boylston was so moved by the cures that he deeded the land and the springs
to God, which allows the springs to remain free to the public. Boylston's deed
reads, "I should return to God the most treasured piece of this earth that I have
ever owned and possessed."

Many of the faithful will swear they've been cured of everything from lower back
pain to heart conditions, and a few will take a blood oath and swear that if people
are baptized in the Healing Springs stream or drink from the 12 spouts that never
stop running, they won't backslide to their former ways. Hopefully, since Blackville
is truly off the beaten path, maybe the *National Enquirer* will leave it alone. As for
me, I kept my right hand in the stream for five full minutes, hoping to soften it up
at impact on my tee shots and turn my hooks into fades.

While you are in town, you can eat a fine meal at a reasonable price at **Miller's
Bread Basket,** 483 Main St., Blackville. For more information on the springs and
Miller's Bread Basket, call (803) 284-3117. This town is so small that everybody
knows everybody.

Due east about 20 miles from Springfield on Highway 4 is Aiken, which
is best known for its thoroughbred horses, its polo teams, and the ***Willcox
Inn*** at 100 Colleton Ave. In the inn's lobby you'll see the two huge stone
fireplaces in front of which Franklin Roosevelt and Winston Churchill sat
during World War II watching the fire, drinking brandy, and wondering

what their next move should be. These boys knew a good thing when they saw it. This inn/spa/retreat is very posh and thoroughly worthwhile. Call (803) 648-1898 or visit thewillcox.com for more information.

The *Aiken County Historical Museum* at 433 Newberry St. is an enormous 17,500-square-foot house built to display a series of rooms furnished in turn-of-the-20th-century style. It also displays agricultural equipment and old firefighting units and has a natural history room. There's an 1808 log cabin, a miniature circus room, and even a 1950s-era drugstore. It is open Tues through Sat from 10 a.m. to 5 p.m. and Sun from 2 to 5 p.m. Admission is free, but donations are appreciated. Call (803) 642-2015 or visit aiken countyhistoricalmuseum.org.

If the *Palmetto Golf Club,* located right in the center of Aiken, isn't the oldest course in the country, it's close. Twelve identical rocking chairs sit on the porch overlooking the first tee and 18th green—the way they have been sitting since the clubhouse was built in 1902 by none other than Evelyn Nesbit's lover, Stanford White. White was also the man who designed the Shinnecock clubhouse, Madison Square Garden, and Grand Central Station. The course itself was remodeled by Alister MacKenzie, the same Scotsman who built the Augusta National, Royal Melbourne, and Cypress Point out in California. Many of the pros stop off at Palmetto for a practice round before they play in the Masters, which is right over the Savannah River a few miles away. In the pro shop is a 1984 photograph of Tom Moore, the pro here, giving Ben Crenshaw some spiritual advice on putting. Crenshaw went on to win the Masters that year, and he's been coming back to see Tom Moore and play Palmetto every year since. He won it again in 1995. Palmetto is a private course, but if you know a pro who knows Tom Moore, there's always a chance you can play here. If you know someone who knows Ben Crenshaw, that would be even better. If you don't golf, this is still a great place to visit. Call (803) 649-2951. There's more about this club's history at palmettogolfclub.net.

A few miles north of Springfield is the town of Salley, the home of the annual *Chitlin Strut,* which is an extravaganza that would be sinful to miss. And what is a chitlin? A Low Country historian is credited with the immortal line, "A chitlin is better discussed than described." Anatomically, they are the intestines of the hog, which normally are used as sausage casings or ground up into lunch meat and hot dogs. Some folks eat them as a dish in themselves. Some even eat a lot of them and actually enjoy them. The long tubelike affair is stretched out and scraped down, turned inside out and scraped again. Then it is stump whipped. Three lengths are braided together, boiled until tender, battered, deep-fat fried, and served. At Salley in late November, as many as five, six, or seven tons of chitlins are served and eaten. One old-time cook said, "Lord, we'd never cook them things here in the summertime. That smell would kill every green thing growing."

During the "boil down" part of the process, no buzzards circle Salley, and no jackals stalk the live oaks and the scrub pine. Small dogs whine and cringe, and large ones head for the corn and bean rows to escape the suffocating stench that hangs in the air—impenetrable, insoluble, incredible. An outsider once moaned, "How do ya'll stand it?" The cook answered, "You get so you get used to it. Go sit in the car and turn the air conditioner on. You don't look so good."

During the Strut the town is packed with 10,000 to 20,000 people all lined up for the hot, greasy fare. They eat and drink beer and lemonade all day and ignore the politicians. Then they hang around for the parade, the beauty pageant, and the high point of the night, the Chitlin Strut Dance Contest. One heavyset dancer I watched one year introduced himself to the crowd as he came shimmy-walking down the center aisle. When he got to the stage, he vaulted over the plastic rhododendron and whipped off an epileptic mountain clog dance that stopped just short of a serious seizure and put the judges in his pocket. Then, swishing his generous hips from side to side, he grinned over his shoulder at the screaming crowd and established one immutable law of the Chitlin Strut: It is not a thin man's dance. It requires bulk, displacement, a stomach, and a rear view of hips, loins, and other choice cuts that a thin man or woman cannot provide. He won the contest hands down and ruled supreme for four straight years.

As with the frog jump, the day of the Strut changes every year, but it's always in late November. Since there are no places to stay in Salley, unless you want to sleep on the ground or in your car, it's best if you get a room in Columbia or over in Aiken. But stay someplace because this is something you'll never, ever forget. Bring your camera. Like the old cook says, "Man, all we have is fun down in here." For information phone (803) 258-3485. There's even an official website; it's chitlinstrut.com.

Places to Stay in the Fall Line

BENNETTSVILLE

Breeden Inn Bed & Breakfast
404 E. Main St.
(843) 479-3665
breedeninn.com

CAMDEN

The Bloomsbury Inn
1707 Lyttleton St.
(803) 432-5858
bloomsburyinn.com

Places to Eat in the Fall Line

CAMDEN

Old Armory Steakhouse
514 Rutledge St.
(803) 432-3222
oldarmorysteakhouse.com

REMBERT

Boykin Company Grille and Store
81 Boykin Mill Rd.
(803) 432-0076
boykinmillfarms.com

Lilfred's
8425 Camden Hwy.
(803) 432-8750
lifreds.net

Mill Pond Steakhouse
84 Boykin Mill Rd.
(803) 425-8825
boykinmillfarms.com

RIDGEWAY

The Thomas Company
105 N. Palmer St.
(803) 337-8594
laurastearoom.com

Blue Ridge Foothills

Open your eyes for new terrain and distant panoramas as you enter the Uplands. The land north and northwest of Aiken changes dramatically from low, flat pastureland to lush foothills of the Blue Ridge Mountains and finally to the mountains themselves, which rise to more than 3,500 feet. West of Aiken are the ***J. Strom Thurmond Dam*** and the ***J. Strom Thurmond Lake.*** If this isn't enough Strom Thurmond for you, you can go 20 miles northwest to ***Edgefield,*** where you can see him striding manfully in bronze in the middle of the town square; this is his home. Edgefield is a beautiful town built around a classic courthouse and a small formal square. It has been home to nine South Carolina governors as well as governor and US senator J. Strom Thurmond, who retired at age 100 after 48 years in the Senate.

The most famous trial at the courthouse here was the one of Becky Cotton, born in 1780. She killed her first husband by running a mattress needle through his heart; she poisoned her second; and she split the head of her third with an ax. The trial was even more interesting than the

murders. While the evidence of her guilt was overwhelming, her beauty was too much for the judge and the jury. Not only was she acquitted, one of the jurymen became her fourth husband.

Later, the author Mason Locke Weems seized on the story for one of his moral pamphlets, "The Devil in Petticoats," or "God's Revenge Against Husband Killing." From his quill we read, ". . . Mrs. Cotton came off clear—nay, more than clear—she came off the conqueror. For as she stood at the bar in tears, with cheeks like rosebuds wet with morning dew and rolling her eyes of sapphires, pleading for pity, their subtle glamour seized with ravishment the admiring bar—the stern features of justice were all relaxed, and both judge and jury hanging forward from their seats breathless, were heard to exclaim, 'Heaven! What a charming creature!'"

East on Highway 23 for a couple miles and then up Highway 121 for 40 miles through some very fine pastureland, you'll come to **Newberry,** home of **Newberry College.** Along with the college you'll find whole blocks of

TOP RECOMMENDATIONS IN UPLANDS & COLUMBIA

Cafe and Then Some
101 College St.
Greenville
(864) 232-2287
cafeats.com

Chattooga National Wild and Scenic River

Francis Beidler Forest
336 Sanctuary Rd.
Harleyville
(843) 462-2150
beidlerforest.audubon.org

Goatfeathers Coffee Bar & Restaurant
2017 Devine St.
Columbia
(803) 256-3325

Riverbanks Zoo and Garden
500 Wildlife Pkwy.
Columbia
(803) 779-8717
riverbanks.org

South Carolina State Museum
301 Gervais St.
Columbia
(803) 898-4921
museum.state.sc.us

Trustus Theater
520 Lady St.
Columbia
(803) 254-9732
trustus.org

historic buildings dating from the 1800s. The college and many of the homes are listed on the National Register of Historic Places. There's more on Newberry College at newberry.edu.

On Main Street, right in the heart of the old town, is the **Old Newberry Courthouse,** which is now a community hall. The flamboyant relief on the front of the building—an eagle with a palmetto tree in its clutches—symbolizes the federal government's hold on South Carolina during Reconstruction. For further information about the history here and a tour of Newberry College, go to the **Newberry County Chamber of Commerce** at 1209 Caldwell St., or call (803) 276-4274. Their website is newberrycounty.org.

Just down the street is Newberry's pride and joy and reason for celebrating—**The Newberry Opera House.** It was originally built in 1882, but over the years it had deteriorated to the point where it had to be closed. After an extensive renovation, costing more than $4 million, it had a gala opening with the South Carolina Philharmonic performing Beethoven, Bach, and Handel as well as George Gershwin. Camelia Johnson and Kevin Maynor of the Metropolitan Opera were also on stage as well as Hal Holbrook and Dixie Carter. The house has 426 seats and in the past has hosted everyone from Lionel Barrymore to cowboy acts. Nicholas Smith, conductor of the South Carolina Philharmonic, and one of the planners for recent events—which range from opera to "opry"—is very excited about the future. He said, "There's no question, it's going to work; of course it's going to work. There's too much good will, good feelings, good effort for it not to." And time has proven him right.

A few years ago much of downtown was crumbling and on the verge of falling down. But with the renovated opera house, the centerpiece, the old town has come back to life. Art galleries, antiques shops, and restaurants now line the once-deserted streets and, what is even more important, above the stores people have moved into apartments. For tickets or more information, write Opera House, Box 357, Newberry 29108; call (803) 276-6264; or visit newberryoperahouse.com. The building alone is worth a visit.

Five minutes from downtown Newberry is the **Carter and Holmes Nursery** at 629 Mendenhall Rd., where you can see some of the finest orchids in the Southeast on display and for sale. There is no admission charge, and the range and variety of orchids in the greenhouses are nothing less than stunning. Open from 9 a.m. to 5 p.m. Mon through Sat. Call (803) 276-0579. You can even order online at carterandholmes.com.

Dining is best done 7 or 8 miles away down Highway 17 in Prosperity at the *Main Dish Cafe.* I had the "rolled" burger, as in rolled in a house-blended seasoning before going on the grill, and it was divine. They also do a great job with sandwiches offering choices like Reubens, Phillys, Cubans, and French dips. I'm partial to their homemade pimento cheese and chicken salad. From the looks of the next table's dessert plates, I'm also getting some brownies and chocolate cake to go next time. They also do a healthy breakfast business among the locals. Slow down and savor the small town atmosphere here. Open Tues and Wed from 7 a.m. to 4 p.m. and Thurs through Sat from 7 a.m. to 9 p.m. Closed Sun and Mon. Call (803) 364-4590.

South of Newberry on Highway 121, turn right on Highway 34 and go about 24 miles to Greenwood, the home of *Park Seed Company,* which is the largest and oldest family-owned mail-order seed company in America. Located at 3507 Cokesbury Rd., Hodges (864-223-8555), the garden shop and the enormous greenhouses are open from 9:30 a.m. to 6 p.m. Mon through Sat in the spring and summer. More than 70,000 plants are planted in the trial gardens here and can be seen seasonally. One of the best times to visit is during the *Festival of Flowers Show* in June; guided tours and horticultural talks are offered on Park Seed Flower Day one Saturday during the festival. Their colorful website is parkseed.com.

Twelve miles west of Greenwood and perched on a series of small hills is my favorite small town, *Abbeville.* Centered around a good-size square and dominated by the tall, thin spire of Trinity Church, the old low-skyline town looks as if it has been here forever. Much work has gone into the preservation of downtown. Everywhere you look, from the hardware store to the drugstore to the poolroom to the Opera House, you realize this is exactly the way the old town was built, and it's exactly the way people here are going to make sure it stays. This is a joy to see.

A wonderful place to stay right in the middle of town is *Veranda On Main* at 802 W. Main St. This bed-and-breakfast is in a majestic Southern Greek Revival–style home with four large and comfortable bedrooms all decorated with a touch of luxury. Innkeepers Thom and Linda Tyner seem to have thought of everything with the private baths, Jacuzzi tub, guest kitchenette, and office space included here. Start your day with their

A Very Short History of South Carolina Football

Right smack in the middle of the dog days of September, when the northern transplants are wondering when, and if, the summer will ever end, the madness begins.
We break out our Gamecock jackets, caps, and banners, and start politicking for a
parking space within 1,000 yards of Williams-Brice Stadium. And then it's Saturday
and there we are, where we've been sitting forever, watching Gamecock football.
The game goes on and the stouthearted fans of 10, 20, 30—you name it—years
cheer and shout, groan and scream all the way into the fourth quarter (even in the
days when we were 14 or 21 or 27 or 36 points behind). Talk about a loyal fan
base!

Looking down the 120-year-old Spanish moss–draped tunnel of Gamecock football,
there is one grim and comic statistic that is seldom reported by the local press. Our
best year (until 1984) was 1903—seven wins and three losses. But one of the victo-
ries was against the Columbia-based YMCA and the other, an 89 to 0 humiliation of
the Welsh Neck High School.

But all this started to change in 1984, when we won five in a row and were rated up
there with the name brands in the Associated Press Poll. I covered the games that
year, and here are the notes from my journal: "Back in the not-so-long-ago days of
'83, '82, '81, and '80, right about now we'd be three wins and three losses, and
we'd be looking forward to basketball and the winter solstice. But this year was different. This was too crazy to believe. We actually had a football team. We'd always had
a football team, but this one was winning. We were actually undefeated in five straight
games and were right up there on page one of the sports section in the *New York
Times,* the *L.A. Times,* and the *Chicago Tribune.* Right up there with Nebraska, Oklahoma, Texas, Ohio State: schools with ball teams that get on national television and
go to bowl games. Schools where the old grads die and leave oil wells and skyscrap-
ers and coastlines to the Athletic Department. Serious big time, household names like
Michigan, Penn State, Southern Cal, and Notre Dame."

But now we were winning. The fever had hit Columbia, and we were twisting and
trembling in torment. New and terrible, weird things were happening all over town—
we were out of control. Housebreaking and embezzling and brutal crimes dipped
20 to 25 points, but freak accidents increased by 30. Cars were piling into hedges,
phone poles, and runoff culverts; others simply left the road as if "The Rapture" was
upon them, and they could be seen out in the fresh rows of collards and soybeans.

But it wasn't The Rapture or the fear of a first strike by the Red Menace, poised somewhere down there in the jungles of Guadalajara. It was pure, cold-biscuit-down-in-the-dirt Gamecock Fear. Our next game was with Notre Dame at Notre Dame, and if by some miracle we won, we would have six wins in a row and be among the top three in the country. At the bars, prayer groups, and Tupperware parties, you could feel the fear. You could hear it.

"Hell, I'm breaking out in a Gamecock Rash."

"I need four drinks to feel one."

"My teeth feel soft and the back of my hands itch."

And one howling looper at the end of the bar banged on it two times, three times, four. "I've had it. You hear me? I can't go on like this! I'm calling Jim Holderman and I'm telling him to stop the damn season and send me the bill."

Anyhow, we beat Notre Dame, then NC State, then Florida State, and were eight in a row with no losses and right up there at number two in the AP Poll. We lost the next game to Navy, but then we beat Clemson and went down to the Gator Bowl, where we lost in the last minute to Oklahoma State. The season ended with nine wins and two losses—the best season yet.

Then there really wasn't too much to crow about until after the Cocks wised up and joined the storied SEC in 1992. Now, I want you to get it in your mind that the SEC is serious football. Very serious. In 1999 Coach Lou Holtz united the flock of 80,000 die-hard fans still showing up every Saturday despite a 0–11 start to his first season. Then Ol' Lou got it turned around and Carolina was in the right place at the right time when Steve Spurrier was looking for work and Lou wanted to retire. Under Spurrier's visor-tossing leadership, the football program has achieved new heights, winning the SEC Eastern Division in 2010 and finishing with 11 wins in 2011, ranking in the final top 10.

And why am I telling you all this? I'll tell you why. Now the Gamecocks are winning and winning big. And the best part is being able to scream out, "How 'bout those Cocks!" without getting arrested. So call the Athletic Department at (803) 777-4274 for the schedule and tickets, and come on out to Williams-Brice. You'll never, ever forget it. If you can't get through, try gamecocksonline.com/tickets.

gourmet Southern breakfast, and you will need (not only want) to spend the day strolling around Abbeville's square and historic sites. After your explorations, the rocking chairs on the veranda welcome you back "home" to sit a spell. A short walk away is the ***Abbeville Opera House,*** so call the inn at (864) 366-9540 or (864) 391-1842 to find out the performance schedule for the Opera House, then book a room around your favorite play or musical. Rates for rooms are from $119 to $149 per night. For more information visit verandaonmain.com.

The Abbeville Opera House doesn't have a bad seat in the place and is absolutely stunning. If you're simply passing through town and seeing a show is not possible, just stop and stick your head in. (It's open for self-guided tours weekdays from 8:30 a.m. to 5 p.m.) You'll be amazed at the size of the enormous stage and the beautiful construction of the balcony. This is probably one of the best-designed theaters in the country, and the Abbevillians take great pride in bringing first-class productions to it year in and year out. The acting and directing talent comes from all over the Southeast, but much of it is from right here in Abbeville County. For reservations and a theater schedule, call the Opera House at (864) 366-2157 between 10 a.m. and 2 p.m. Mon through Fri, or check out theabbeville operahouse.com.

Beautiful hills, lakes, and horse and cattle country lie northwest of Abbeville as the land rises into the foothills of the Blue Ridge Mountains. But, frankly, there isn't much to do but look at it. The best stop between Abbeville and Clemson is the town of Pendleton. And the best stop here is the bed-and-breakfast ***Liberty Hall Inn,*** at 621 S. Mechanic St. This is a circa 1840 family home that has been rebuilt and restored and is now one of the best bed-and-breakfasts in the state. The rooms are large, with high ceilings and heart pine floorboards, and are furnished in antiques. Each room has air-conditioning, a telephone, a television, Wi-Fi, and a private bath. Rates are $150 to $170 per night, with a plated gourmet breakfast. If you're not staying here, you can always eat here. Dinner is served from 5 to 9 p.m. Tues through Sat. Lunch is served from 11 a.m. to 2 p.m. Tues through Fri. Prices are $14 to $26. The wine list is impressive, and other spirits are, of course, available. Call (864) 502-2228. Don't try to stay here during the football season—it's booked solid. There's more information at libertyhallinn.com.

While you're in the Pendleton area, you're too close to Clemson not to drive through and look over the ***Clemson University*** campus, which features great redbrick buildings, rolling hills, and beautiful trees. The school is famous for textile engineering, architecture, and the liberal arts, and many of its graduates are employed by the big international firms in Greenville and Spartanburg a few miles away. Clemson is also famous for its football, basketball, soccer, and baseball teams. There's more on Clemson at clemson.edu.

As a matter of fact, you'll need some luck if you want to see a football game. Despite the fact that the stadium holds 80,000, seats can be hard to come by. But for the dedicated, there is a way. Don't go to the stadium; go to the ***Esso Club*** and just stand around—something will happen. It could be a fight, someone might pass out, or die . . . as I said, something. But hang around long enough, and you'll get a ticket. Read more lore about this place at theessoclub.com.

footballmania (clemsontigers)

Coon Williams, a local scribe, once said, "Some anthropologists maintain that Clemson tailgating is a cultural event comparable to the 'Chitlin Strut' and the 'Springfield Frog Jump.' But I say there is nothing out there on the boards as outrageous as 80,000 Clemson fans shrink-wrapped in orange (the school color) eating and drinking, listening to taped highlights of the '81 season (the year they won the National Championship), and their 'Tiger Rag' auto horns blaring and standing in line for the Port-O-Johns—and that's why I love them." Here ends the chronicle.

Thirty miles northeast of Pendleton is the tiny crossroads town of Salem. The best way here is up Highway 11, but you'll have to watch for the signs. A mile out of town on a high-rising hill—you are now in the high foothills of the Blue Ridge Mountains—is the ***Sunrise Farm Bed & Breakfast*** at 325 Sunrise Dr. The guest rooms are nicely appointed with period antiques, thick comforters, and family heirlooms. Large windows provide wonderful views of the mountains. This area is famous for hiking and rafting on the nearby Chattooga River. Rates run from $105 to $195 per night, including breakfast. For reservations and further information, call (888) 991-0121. Their website is sunrisefarmbb.com.

Tigers versus Gamecocks

You'd need a phone-book-thick volume and a 10-hour miniseries to even touch the lore, the action, and the downright insanity of college football down here. First of all, the number one game—and it's the day the state shuts down—is between the Clemson Tigers and the University of South Carolina Gamecocks, a game that goes back to the beginning of time. Tickets are impossible to get. Many are passed on in wills, others are divided up during divorces and right over the graves at funerals, while others are bought on the open market for the price you'd pay for a good used car.

Most people don't even try to get tickets. Some arrive at Clemson Stadium and park their Winnebago near the walls, open their chaise lounges, plug in their TV sets, and turn on the radio. Radio announcers are not only much better down here than TV announcers, they know the players and their families and, if pushed, can come up with exactly where they live and the name of their dogs.

The spokesman for one group who had gathered at Clemson put everything in perspective: "Friend, what if we got four sets of tickets—which we won't anyhow—but say we did just for argument's sake. First of all we'd have to split up, and we don't want to do that. We've been together for 12 years now. This way we stay together, we don't have to fight the crowd, we can drink all the beer we want, and the john's right here. Hell, all our friends know we're here, and they all come by for some barbecue and pimento cheese. And I'll tell you something else. When the Tigers score and that noise goes up and the old stadium starts rocking, I wouldn't trade this spot for eight box seats with the Board of Trustees."

On the shores of Lake Jocassee, which many consider the most beautiful lake in the state, is **Devils Fork State Park** at 161 Holcombe Circle, Salem. Built in cooperation with Duke Power Company, it is managed by the Division of State Parks. Twenty luxurious mountain villas, 59 campsites, swimming facilities, boat ramps, and picnic areas are available. Day admission is only $2. For more information and reservations, call (864) 944-2639 or see southcarolinaparks.com/devilsfork.

From Salem a nice trip would be northeast to Sassafras Mountain, which is 3,533 feet and the highest point in South Carolina. This is a wild and beautiful part of the state, and some of the vistas out over the mountains and valleys look a great deal like Scotland. Driving here at night, you'll be amazed how bright the stars are. You'll also be surprised by how few lights you see.

The Greenville Area

Many small cities boast of a renaissance in their downtown areas, but few have delivered on the claim like *Greenville.* It could be her sister-city relationship with Bergamo, Italy, that made the city planners take the concept as seriously as they have, but more than 10 years of effort have made a difference that few could have imagined. You can get a nice overview of Greenville at greenville.com.

The new downtown is a showpiece anchored by the restored *Westin Poinsett Hotel,* with restaurants, coffee shops, sidewalk cafes, and lots of things to do and places to see—all in walking distance of one another. Feeling bookish? Or maybe you want to see an outstanding art exhibition? How about taking in a play? You can find what you want all in an area of two city blocks at *Heritage Green,* home to the county library, the Little Theatre, and the *Greenville Museum of Art.*

The *Greenville County Library* is bright and spacious (designers have made exceptional use of glass throughout) and includes a coffee shop; a large video, CD, audio book, and e-book center; and a noncirculating research collection of South Carolina history and culture. You can check them out at greenvillelibrary.org or call them at (864) 242-5000. Next door to the library, the *Greenville Little Theatre* (greenvillelittletheatre.org or 864-233-6238) features regular first-rate productions (Joanne Woodward is an alumna, after all), and just one door from the theater is the Greenville Museum of Art, for years the home of the Wyeth Collection and still showing pieces by many nationally and world-renowned artists. If you happen to be a fan of Andrew Wyeth's work, you'll be very impressed with this museum's collection. Emphasizing his watercolor portraits and landscapes, the Wyeth collection represents every phase of the artist's storied career. Wyeth himself called it "the very best collection of my watercolors in any public museum in this country." But there's also a nice collection of Impressionist art here, and they always have a timely and uplifting traveling exhibit up and ready to enjoy. This is a "hidden" gem you don't want to miss, and admission is free. You can write them at 420 College St., Greenville 29601, or call (864) 271-7570. There's much more on the Greenville Museum of Art at greenvillemuseum.org.

A block away is the local favorite, *Cafe and Then Some* at 101 College St. The "Cafe" part refers to their menu with a touch of fun offering

Trailer Park Ribs, Scallop Pot Pie, and Chocolate Peanut Butter Bomb. The "Then Some" part covers the Wed through Sat night shows of folksy satire and music. Proprietors Bill and Susan Smith take on the roles of "Bubba" and "Norma Jean, a big ole country and western star" in the performances. Dinner-and-show seating is from 6:30 to 7:30 p.m., and show-only seating is at 7:45 p.m. Call (864) 232-CATS or go to cafeats.com to make a reservation.

One block up and a right turn (still walking) and you are on Main Street, at the hub of the downtown renewal. The other anchor of the area, **The Hyatt Regency,** invites you into a glass atrium, with restaurant and bar, the perfect start to an evening. Moving down Main Street, you will find eateries, bistros, tobacco and clothing stores, and gift shops. As you walk through **Bergamo Square,** you will find that many of the restored buildings are home to new residents of the downtown area, remodeled walk-up flats that are also just a walk away from the office. During the spring and summer months, as well as early fall, live bands give free concerts in the square every Fri, and downtown festivals celebrating almost any occasion regularly turn the area into the upstate's largest block party.

Your next stop, only three blocks down from the square on Main Street, is **The Peace Center,** a gem of a concert hall that was built in 1989 and named after one of its primary benefactors. The center is a regular draw for touring Broadway musicals, concerts, and solo artists. It was also the site in 2004 for one of the nationally televised Democratic primary presidential debates; the moderator, NBC's Tom Brokaw, was so impressed, the evening news for that night was anchored from the center. The Peace Center is also part of a pavilion that includes restaurants, banquet facilities, and an open-air forum for speakers, artists, and social functions. Check out peacecenter .org or call (864) 467-3000.

Baseball fans take note: The city is home to the Class A minor-league baseball team (and Boston Red Sox affiliate) **Greenville Drive.** The team's home stadium is located just off of West Main, and provides ample parking for fans in county office spaces only two blocks away. For those not up for a walk, trams run every 10 minutes to deliver you to the front gate of the stadium. If you want to leave early, stop for dinner at the **Brick Street Cafe,** 315 Augusta St., and order a bowl of gumbo—one of the daily specials—and top it off with a generous piece of carrot or pineapple cake and a cup of cinnamon coffee. Call (864) 421-0111 or check them out at brickstreetcafe.com.

If you have ever been to Fenway Park, you may feel a sense of déjà vu when you enter Fluor Field at the West End. No surprise there: The Drive is a part of the Boston Red Sox organization, and the ballpark is a remarkable replica of the field in Boston, down to Greenville's own version of the fabled Green Monster in left field. Ticket prices at the stadium, as well as prices for the hot dogs, barbecue, popcorn, and beer, are also a welcome throwback to the days when a family of four or a couple wanting to spend a night watching America's pastime could do it all without breaking the bank. Call the box office at (864) 240-4528 or visit milb.com/tickets to get your seats.

Just across from the front gate is the **Shoeless Joe Jackson Museum** at 356 Field St., housed in the home of the baseball great claimed by both Pickens County (where he was born) and Greenville (where he played textile-league baseball and spent his later years). Baseball fans won't want to miss this one—just follow the bare feet footprints around to the side door. See shoelessjoejackson.org for hours and details.

trivia

At the Greenville welcome center, there is a water tower painted to resemble a baseball in remembrance of ballplayer Shoeless Joe Jackson of the 1919 Black Sox.

The Haywood Road area is the heart of what the locals call the Eastside, with malls, restaurants, bookstores, shopping—all minutes from four hotels just off I-385. In the mood for steaks, drinks, and good company? Try **John Paul's Armadillo Oil Company Inc.,** a cross between a tavern and a hunting lodge at 637 Congaree Rd. (864-288-8607), for good, casual dining at reasonable prices ($15 to $25 per person, with an appetizer). If you lived in the upstate or across the line in Charlotte during the early 1960s, you might listen closely when you meet your host, owner and operator John Paul, usually there greeting friends, regulars, and newcomers, all with the same warm handshake and raspy voice. The sound of that voice should be familiar, and suddenly you just might hear music, like maybe the Temptations, the Tams, or the Four Tops. In the golden '60s, you knew the voice of John Paul as the nighttime disc jockey on WAYS in Charlotte, Long John Silver (he still wears the familiar black eye patch). He was the one who kept you posted, with his Super Wonder Dog Blue, on the latest in pop music and the results just in from folks parked out at the airport watching the submarine races. John Paul's website is johnpauls.com.

If you're looking for something different, try the buffalo steak at *Saskatoon Steaks, Fish and Wildgame,* 477 Haywood Rd. (864-297-7244). Or have something hot and bubbly at *The Melting Pot,* a fondue restaurant at 475 Haywood Rd. (864-297-5035), or hot and spicy at *Chili's Grill and Bar,* 490 Haywood Rd. (864-281-0547). For breakfast, try *Stax's Omega,* known for Greek omelettes made with feta cheese and spinach, Greek toast, and home-fried potatoes, with coffee, all for under $10. They are located at 72 Orchard Park Dr. (864-297-6639).

At the end of the evening, you may just want to read the paper and enjoy a cup of coffee and something sweet. Drop by *Barnes & Noble Bookstore* at 735 Haywood Rd. (864-458-9113) or *Books-a-Million* at 2465 Laurens Rd. (864-281-1301). Yes, I know, they are national chains, but the people are local, the food and coffee are really good, and although you're in a strange city, the feeling is one of a large coffeehouse with a lot of great books and magazines, and friends waiting to be introduced. All you have to do is start the conversation by mentioning something interesting you've read lately.

If you're staying anywhere on the Eastside off I-85 (maybe going north to Charlotte or south to "Hotlanta"), then the Pelham Road area may offer some easy dining choices, once you decide which of the many is for you. Most are chains, and most are located off E. Beacon Road (or E. Beacon Drive, coming the other way), the Eastside's restaurant row. The food is good at any of them.

Want Italian? Stop in at *Romano's Macaroni Grill,* 105 E. Beacon Dr. (864-675-6676). For seafood, there's *Joe's Crab Shack*, 102 E. Beacon Dr. (864-987-0009); for Mexican, there's *On the Border Mexican Grill and Cantina,* 74 Beacon Dr. (864-214-2260); and for a little bit of everything fixed just right, try *California Dreaming,* 40 Beacon Dr. (864-234-9000). All of these offer very good meals at prices generally in a range of $15 to $20 per person, within a two-minute drive from the Greenville-Spartanburg Airport Marriott Hotel and within walking distance of each other.

The crown jewel of restaurant row is *Chophouse 47,* 36 Beacon Dr. (864-286-8700 or chophouse47.com), an excellent choice for fine dining and drinks. The service is terrific, and you might dress up a bit for the evening, a dining experience worth the price ($50 and up per person, with wine or cocktails), if you want to do it right. For more on Greenville's restaurant row, visit greenvillecvb.com.

It's all about barbecue in South Carolina, a state where the Uplands claim a ketchup base is the only way to go, the Midlands claim a mustard base is the only way, and the Low Country claims a vinegar base is . . . well, you get the idea. **Little Pigs Bar-B-Q** offers chopped barbecue prepared daily, regular and jumbo sandwiches and plates, with hush puppies, corn on the cob, and fries on the side. You can get a sandwich for $3.89, a basket for $6.49, and feed the family with a chopped half pound for $8.25. Located at 522 Mills Ave.; call (864) 235-7211.

You wanna play pool or billiards? If the latter, spend a coupla grand and get your own table, but if it's pool you want, **The Corner Pocket** is the place. It has been renovated and is more upscale than when a former governor was a teenager first learning the hustle (our kind, not that disco stuff), but it is still the place downtown where you can rack 'em and play by the hour. The bar is friendly, and the menu has some good appetizers and lunch plates. Reasonably priced, especially if you talked that kid who just walked through the door into a game of eight ball, loser pays. The Corner Pocket Tavern and Oyster Bar is at 21 E. Coffee St.; (864) 242-3432.

Beano Brothers Coffee and Cafe is definitely not on the beaten path, at least not for those looking for a cup of coffee and something to eat during the morning rush. But it is located without fanfare in the much-traveled Pelham Road area of Greenville. It offers good coffee and a gathering spot for mornings and afternoons during the week, and lunch Mon through Sat. Try the crumb cake or cinnamon roll weekdays with a cup of Beano Blend for breakfast, and for lunch a Papa's Pollo or Mama's Seta followed by a cappuccino grande. Lunch is under $10. It's at 4 Independence Pointe, behind the Observatory (864-675-0303); takeout is available.

"The best steaks around downtown." A lot of native Greenvillians will tell you that's what's waiting at **Charlie's Steak House,** a Greenville touchstone for great food in a casual, friendly atmosphere. Your steak is cooked to order with baked or fried potatoes, bread, and a salad. You'll find yourself in a true old-fashioned steak house when you step from the curb through the door at 18 E. Coffee St. Dinner with a drink will run around $25. Call (864) 232-9541 or visit charliessteakhouseonline.com.

Trio Brick Oven Cafe is a downtown favorite for lunch or dinner, located at 22 N. Main St., the corner of Main and Coffee. The service is good and the menu is distinctive, with lots of Italian dishes and a sampling from the South to choose from. Generous servings of the penne-goat pasta or the baked chicken (with skin or skinless) with Yukon Gold potatoes will leave you ready for a walk through the downtown sights. Lunch or dinner with a glass of wine will run about $10 to $20 per person. There's more at triocafe .com, or call them at (864) 467-1000.

Greenville has some excellent coffeehouses, and not just the standard franchise variety. ***Coffee Underground*** is at 1 E. Coffee St. This is not just another Mickey D's. Comfortable sofas and chairs are arranged for relaxed conversation, giving you time to enjoy your cup with a piece of strawberry cake, cheesecake, or any number of other good choices. Or go ahead and just order a decaf—they'll know you're not a regular, but they'll still let you drink it at your own pace and enjoy the movie (yep, they have them free more than occasionally). Call (864) 298-0494 or see coffeeunderground.biz.

Nick and Iris Tassopoulos have a good thing going. They know it and so does anybody who eats at ***Never on Sunday Greek Restaurant,*** located at 210 E. Coffee St. in downtown Greenville. Lunch or dinner, the food is always excellent, the service outstanding (Iris serves while Nick mans the kitchen), and there is always something on the menu that is truly Greek and truly great. The two-room dining area is cozy and casual, decorated with a touch of the old country and photos of friends, old and new. They can handle appetites from 2 to 10 at one sitting, with a menu that goes from the standard favorite, moussaka, to other more special dishes, to be accompanied by a glass of wine or the best iced tea in the upstate (Iris has a secret to preparing it—ask and she might tell you, if she decides you're a friend). Be sure and order the baklava for dessert, but you have to eat it with your fingers (Iris can tell if you are going to be a regular or just passing through by this little test). Lunch or dinner for around $10 to $20 per person; call (864) 232-2252.

Travinia Italian Kitchen is located at 1625 Woodruff Rd. Opened in 2003, it has become one of the best Italian restaurants in the greater Greenville area, with a menu that has familiar dishes like pasta (angel hair Bolognese, sausage and peppers rustica, and home-style cannelloni), as well as salads that everybody knows (a great Caesar) or some that you have to try

(Belgian endive and Granny Smith apple salad). The portions are generous, and a meal that includes any of these dishes with a glass of wine costs about $20. The bar is a good one, and the atmosphere includes lots of Sinatra, Tony Bennett, and other favorites; easy lighting; and comfortable booths. Coming from Columbia and other places south, take the Woodruff Road exit off I-385, turn right onto Woodruff Road, drive approximately 2 miles, and you are there, on the left. Call (864) 458-8188 or check out travinia.com. Even the photos are delicious.

City Range Steak House Grill is the best thing for appetites near Haywood Mall. And there is a lot going on in either direction when you take the Haywood Road exit from I-385. The area has many good restaurants, but City Range's southwestern decor, view-through fireplace, two dining areas, and intimate bar make it something special. Add to this the fine service and a menu that includes such varied specialties as honey pecan and Gorgonzola salad, butter crumb trout, herb-crusted rib eye, or char-grilled pork chop. Dinner and a drink will be around $30 to $35 per person. Located at 615 Haywood Rd. Call (864) 286-9018 or visit cityrange.com.

If you're looking for good music, dancing, and some company, there is all of that and more at the *Blind Horse Saloon,* a popular watering hole that features new talents on the rise in country music. It's located at 1035 Lowndes Hill Rd. (864-233-1381 or blind-horse.com). In the downtown area there is *The Handlebar,* a club featuring something for almost everyone's choice of music, with a mix of nationally recognized musicians and regional and local talent, folk music balladeers, and hard-rocking Grammy winners. It's at 304 Stone Ave. (864-233-6173 or handlebar-online.com).

The *Peddler Steak House* is a cut above. Reservations are only for parties of 10 or more, but a well-arranged plan for seating and serving, along with a nostalgia-filled bar and seating room, usually makes the wait quick and comfortable. In cold weather, wood fires are kept burning in original stone fireplaces, pleasant reminders that you are dining in a renovated stone and wood farmhouse. The salad bar is excellent, and starts you off until the meat cutter makes his way to your table to offer the cut of steak you choose. Although a menu is posted, most diners prefer the steaks, which bring them back time and time again; dinner with a cocktail will run about $30 to $40 a person. A bargain buy if you go often is the Peddler Card, purch annually for 10 visits. It allows you to buy an entree and enjoy free for your guest. Find it at 2000 Poinsett Hwy. in Greenville. Call (864) 235-7192 or go to thepeddlersteakhouse.com.

Driving all the way out Wade Hampton Boulevard will bring you to another city renovation and revival that has proven that, just like neckties and scarves, sometimes the old becomes new again. The city of **Greer** has worked to restore the downtown area as well as create a civic spirit, which is a bit like sharing a block party with the neighborhood. This means that during the spring, summer, and fall months, on any calendared holiday (and some apparently created just because the weather permitted), there are concerts, shows, or art exhibits in the downtown area, all within a short walk of a few blocks from one another. In the fall of 2006, the city held its first Oktoberfest.

If you want to do a little shopping, the remodeled Old Greer Railway Station serves up some nice possibilities, named collectively and appropriately enough, **The Shops at the Old Greer Station.** A luncheon at the **Southern Thyme Cafe,** 219 Trade St. (864-801-9551 or southernthymescafe .com), or a cup of java at the **Stomping Grounds,** 208 Trade St. (864-334-0115), is a sample of the good life made simple.

At the junction of Highway 14 and Highway 11, at 11250 New Cut Rd., Campobello, you can find a secret, one they know about in a small part of four counties and two states. They call it the **Links O' Tryon,** a semiprivate club that features an 18-hole golf course, an Olympic-size swimming pool (club membership required), and tennis courts. The Links course is set near the foothills of the upstate—18 challenging holes tailored for the shot maker by Tom Jackson, a course architect who started his career under Robert Trent Jones. The clubhouse has a restaurant open to the public that offers lunch including cheeseburgers, Reubens, and Philly steak sandwiches, as well as luncheon and dinner specials and a regular Sunday brunch menu. Lunch will run $7 to $10, brunch around $13, and dinner (served only on We‌ ‌i) $12 to $17 per person. Call (864) 468-4995 or (864) 472-6723, ‌ryongc.com for more information.

‌u're headed down Highway 11 and you come to the cross- ‌nction with Highway 14. This time, you want to go right, ‌o the north. Head up Highway 14 just a few miles and ‌ another junction, where Highway 14 becomes W. ‌hway 176 becomes Howard Street. Across the rail tracks you will find another successful revamping of a downtown, starting at **The Hare & Hound,** a small tavern that local folks will tell you used to be Wilson's Five and Dime, where candy and gum were sold by the piece from large barrels. The address is 101 E. Rutherford St., and the phone is (864) 457-3232.

The upstate of South Carolina is growing, and every year welcomes new and significant additions to its already strong Hispanic communities. One of the nice benefits from this are some excellent restaurants, including **El Chile Rojo,** located in the center of Landrum. The service is excellent, the staff is friendly, and the menu offers a little of everything that you might be familiar with, plus a few dishes that you need to find out about. A meal with tea or coffee runs under $10. The address is 209 E. Rutherford St.; call (864) 457-5977.

After checking out the restaurants and shops in Landrum, drive a few miles farther north on Highway 176 and across the state line to a special treasure: **Tryon,** North Carolina. As you enter Tryon, you pass shops and antiques stores **(The Old Mill Flea Market)** along the way to the downtown square, 8 to 10 blocks that you can browse through at your leisure (free two-hour parking). At **The Shops of Tryon,** a building renovation turned walk-in mall, start at **10 North Trade Street Café** (10northtrade.com or 828-859-3010), offering pastries and very good coffee to take with you on your stroll. Be sure to step into the framing and art galleries on both sides of Trade Street, the antiques shops and bookstores, **Buck's Pizza** (buckspizza .com or 828-859-0400), and **Trade Street Gallery Coffee House** (coffee house.xenei.net or 828-859-0207). If you stay until evening, you can take in a movie. Man, oh man, can you take in a movie.

The **Tryon Theatre** is an original, a landmark, a for-real movie house that dates back to the days of first-run epics like *Ben-Hur* and *Spartacus,* to the times when Doris Day comedies and Alfred Hitchcock suspense thrillers ruled, to the days of musicals and Saturday matinees. The owner and manager, Barry Flood, has preserved a time capsule for film buffs and updated it just enough for the fans of a new era. In spring 2004 he put in new (but still conventional, 1950s-style) seats. The Tryon Film Society meets at the theater to vote on selections the second and fourth Mon and Tues of each month; membership is $12 per year and provides a $1 discount on tickets for each show. Feature presentations are at 8 p.m. Wed through Sat ($6 per person), and there is a matinee on Sun at 3 p.m. ($5). Popcorn and soft drinks come in two sizes, small ($2) and large ($3), with more generous servings than other theaters. If you like, sit in the balcony and choose from the several good beers they offer, or maybe a glass of wine. Want coffee? They've got coffee, from Little River Roasting Company in Spartanburg. Try to put this in perspective, folks: Between the Outer Banks of North Carolina and just about any part of the Gulf Coast, there are two places to find a theater this great—one is in Tryon, and the other is somewhere else. Call (828) 859-6811 or visit tryontheatre.com.

So you've finished your walk through town, had a treat or a beer, picked up something to take home, seen a good movie . . . what next? By now you may want to retire here (that's just what Perry Como did, 7 miles up the road in Saluda)—or at least retire for the night. As Tony Bennett might say, the best is yet to come.

You can stay at **Butterfly Creek Bed & Breakfast Inn** (877-894-6393 or butterflycreekinn.com), which is charmingly comfortable, or if you decide to make it a long weekend, heavy on the romance in style, call ahead for reservations at **The Pine Crest Inn,** up New Market Road from Trade Street, left on Pine Crest Lane. The Pine Crest just may be the finest little hotel of its kind in the Carolinas, a triple-A, four-diamond award winner arranged as a compound of 12 cottages and a main lodge with 35 rooms. The main building was constructed in 1906, then bought by horseman Carter Brown, who converted it into an inn and owned it until it was bought by the current owners, one of whom is Carl Caudle, who also acts as innkeeper.

The main lodge is informal and cozy, decorated in warm colors and furnished with a mix of antique wood and glass curio cupboards, sofas, and tables arranged on hardwood floors covered with fine rugs—ideal places for drinks and conversation in front of two fireplaces. One of the rooms also serves as a bar and small library for reading while you wait for the main event of the evening dinner in the inn's restaurant. The restaurant is all about fine dining, gourmet southern foothills cuisine with a bit of French and Italian as well. Crab cakes made only with fresh lump crabmeat from North or South Carolina and calamari are just two of the appetizers, followed by menu regulars such as lamb chops served with warm goat cheese and red pepper jelly and the filet mignon, only from Black Angus beef, served with a rotation of sauces to keep a regular favorite from becoming routine.

Dessert is prepared by the pastry and bread chef, a graduate of Le Cordon Bleu, and the crème brûlée is only one of the two house specialties. The wine cellar has more than 1,500 labels. Dinner for two runs $100 to $150, more with wine (some selections are $500 per bottle).

Reservations for the inn are recommended. During most months, a week ahead is fine to assure availability of a room, suite, or cottage. Spring, summer, and fall are all busy seasons, with Jan, Feb, and Mar generally slower. Rooms are at a premium during the week of the **Block House Steeplechase,** Tryon's annual horse race held in mid-April, unless you make reservations at least one month ahead. Check (800) 633-3001, (828) 859-9135, or pinecrestinn.com for rates, reservations, and more information about rooms, cottages, and availability.

Take Highway 11 to the Cleveland Junction with Highway 276, then turn right and keep going, past the little waterfall on the right where the vendor has her stand selling apples, cider, and coffee. Then bear left at the fork in the road ahead, still on Highway 11, and continue on through the rolling, wooded hills of Pickens County for about 12 miles to the wooden sign ahead on the right that announces **Table Rock State Park.** The lake is on the left all the way up the winding road to the lodge. **Table Rock Lodge** was built by the Civilian Conservation Corps as part of FDR's New Deal, and was one of the many construction projects of the CCC from 1933 through 1942. In the past the lodge was a favorite dining spot for many in Greenville and Pickens Counties, until it closed in March 2004 for remodeling. Restored to its former glory, the lodge is no longer a restaurant but a venue for private events (like weddings and parties) and occasional musical performances. You oughta hear their bluegrass pickin'. Call (864) 878-9813 or visit southcarolinaparks.com/tablerock for scheduling.

You like fresh seafood but you can find it only on the coast, right? Not so. **The Flounder** is a Spartanburg mainstay, a family seafood restaurant along the lines of the old-time fish camp, complete with wooden booths, aluminum trays, and a basic menu that is reasonably priced. The flounder fillet and oyster stew are among the favorites (dinner includes coleslaw, hush puppies, french fries, and tea, all for under $10), served up by a second and third generation of owners and operators from 3:30 until 9:30 p.m., Wed through Sat. There is usually a line by 5 p.m., but fine service and a large dining area help move it quickly. On I-85 north from Greenville, exit numbers have changed with the interstate alterations following the opening of the giant BMW plant in the Midlands area. At the I-85 fork (Charlotte or Spartanburg), take the Spartanburg lane, then the next exit to the stop sign; turn left and then right just after the overpass, and follow the frontage road until you are there, at 160 Barbado Ln. (864-576-3165).

The Peach Region

Until 30 years ago the Midlands area was largely supported by textile mills, cotton, soybeans, tobacco, and a huge peach crop. Now we see a growing industrial revolution, the centerpiece of which is the enormous BMW plant.

Spartanburg, with an elevation of about 900 feet, is in the foothills of the Blue Ridge Mountains. The county and the city get their name from the Spartan Regiment, a body of South Carolina militia that was formed in this area and served with distinction during the American Revolution. Its most noteworthy engagement was at Cowpens, in what was one of the decisive battles of the war.

Today Spartanburg is a surprisingly cosmopolitan city. It has even taken on an international quality. A good example of this change is the very fine *Gerhard's Cafe* at 1200 E. Main St., right on the town square. They feature a menu of German and Austrian entrees as well as seafood, pork, rack of lamb, and pepper steak. Prices range from $17 to $28. Open for dinner Mon through Sat. Call (864) 591-1920 or take a look at gerhardscafe.net.

Seven blocks away on Church Street, with a high hilltop setting of 65 acres or so, are the beautiful old redbrick buildings of *Wofford College,* founded in 1854 and governed by the Methodist Church of South Carolina. The school is internationally known for its program in the liberal arts, especially in English and history. On the campus is a simple granite monument over the graves of Dr. Benjamin Wofford, the founder, and his wife, Anna Todd. The monument bears the same Latin inscription as the grave of Sir Christopher Wren, translated as if you would see this monument, LOOK ABOUT YOU. There's much more about Wofford at wofford.edu.

As you drive northwest from Spartanburg on I-85, the kids will spot the big peach first. It's an enormous one-million-gallon water tower painted like a ripe peach, and it's meant to tell you that you're getting close to *Gaffney,* the home of the ***Gaffney Peach Festival.*** This is peach country—as a matter of cold fact, Spartanburg and Cherokee Counties produce more peaches than all of Georgia. Gaffney, a town of 12,400, is the home of the peach festival, which takes place the first week of July and attracts as many as 300,000 people. For more information, visit scpeachfestival.org. Gaffney is also the home of ***Limestone College,*** the state's oldest institution of higher education for women, founded in 1845 (now coeducational). See more on Limestone at limestone.edu. Here, you'll also find at least a dozen National Register homes that date back to the early 1800s.

Here's a little background on Gaffney. Back in 1835 promoters took over the town and ballyhooed it as the South's Saratoga. This was the heyday of therapeutic mineral treatment, and plantation owners from Charleston and the Low Country, plagued every summer by malaria, flocked here to drink the water, gamble in the casino, and visit the racetrack. Gaffney also became famous for its jousting tournaments, cockfights, and gander pullings (which is the fine but mercifully lost art of snatching off the head of a plucked and greased goose while riding at a hard gallop).

After this medicine-show enterprise failed, Gaffney evolved into a thriving textile mill center until the mill closings of the last 30 or so years. Today, four mills remain, employing about 2,000 workers, and the Nestlé Frozen Food Company and Timken Roller Bearing Company also operate here, but downtown Gaffney has been neglected and allowed to go to seed. One can hope that one day they will follow Greenville's lead and renovate a few of the old buildings, plant some trees, and bring the old town back to life, but in the meantime this is still a good stopover because you can see the beautiful buildings of Limestone and the old homes.

If you want to find the perfect place to get an idea of how an old mill town must have felt not too many years ago, go to ***Harold's Restaurant*** in the heart of downtown Gaffney. It has a four-table poolroom and bar next door, and it does a thriving lunch and short-order business, with prices right out of the 1960s. A chicken salad sandwich, which is very good, is only $2.39; a pint of coleslaw is only $2.99. During the peach festival people line up for the take-out specials—a pint of chicken salad at $5.39, a gallon of chili for $21.99. Reservations aren't needed, but if you want to order over the phone and then pick it up, call (864) 489-9153. The owner, Tony Lipscomb, is very young and very personable and will be glad to tell you about Gaffney and the peach festival. You can't miss Harold's at 602 N. Limehouse St. The website is haroldsrestaurant.com.

Back on I-85 you will see the entrance to Highway 11, also called *Cherokee Foothills Scenic Highway.* If you can spare the time, this beautiful 130-mile road through the heart of the state's Blue Ridge Mountains will take you back to I-85 on the other side of the state. The following are a few of the incredible vistas along the way.

Caesar's Head has been a resort since antebellum times. It features a rock that juts out from the mountainside more than 1,200 feet above the Saluda River valley. Literature and exhibits are available at the visitor center here that describe the natural history of the area, with particular emphasis on the trails systems and the history of the early settlers. Call (864) 836-6115 or see southcarolinaparks.com/caesarshead.

Raven Cliff Falls, located off Highway 276 near Greenville County, is a 420-foot-high cascade in the Mountain Bridge Wilderness and Recreation Area and is one of the most breathtaking waterfalls in South Carolina. A 2-mile hike is necessary to reach the area.

Sassafras Mountain, which stands 3,533 feet high, is the highest point in South Carolina. From the top, four states can be viewed: Tennessee, North Carolina, South Carolina, and Georgia.

The *Chattooga National Wild and Scenic River,* another highlight of the Cherokee Foothills Scenic Highway, is a mecca for whitewater enthusiasts. *Nantahala Outdoor Center* at 13077 Highway 19 West, Bryson City, North Carolina, is licensed to take groups on the Chattanooga River for whitewater excitement. Call (888) 905-7238 for schedules. *Wildwater, Ltd.* proudly announces that they have safely carried more than 300,000 guests on their rafting trips on the Chattooga. Trips on Section III of the Chattooga are perfect for families and youth groups. Section IV is for the more advanced and more adventuresome. Call (828) 488-2176 or check out noc.com for more.

From Gaffney due east on Highways 29 and 5, the next stop is *York,* which was settled by the Scots and the Irish in the 1700s. For a time in the 1920s and 1930s, the Barnett Brothers' Circus made its winter quarters here. Back then every Christmas shopping season was officially opened with a parade in which Santa Claus, escorted by the high school band, came swaying down Congress Street perched high above the crowd on the back of an elephant. Even today, it's said a few of the milky-white dogs of the town are descended from the long line of somersaulting terriers of the old circus.

In any event, York is a unique and charming town. ***The McCelvey Center,*** 212 E. Jefferson St., is a 500-seat performing arts theater and the centerpiece of the community's cultural activities. ***Summerfest,*** a daylong extravaganza of children's activities, craft fairs, a classic car show, and a fire-works display, is held here on the fourth Sat in Aug. It has been designated as one of the top 20 events in the entire Southeast. During the second week-end in Dec, the town hosts ***Christmas in Olde York,*** when the historic houses, of which there are many, are open to visitors and the quaint streets are lit by luminarias for candelight tours. There's more on York's activities at visityorkcounty.com.

York is full of surprises, and one is the ***Museum of York County,*** a few miles east off Highway 161 at 4621 Mount Gallant Rd., Rock Hill. Watch for the museum signs—they'll lead you right there. The museum features the world's largest collection of mounted African hoofed animals, which are displayed in huge dioramas. My favorite is the rampaging elephant, which is rearing up at least 20 feet and swinging its tusks to the sky. Small kids go wild for this one. The museum also has a planetarium and a nature trail. Admission is $5 for adults, $3 for children, and free on Sun. Open Tues through Sat from 10 a.m. to 5 p.m. and Sun from 1 to 5 p.m.; closed major holidays. Call (803) 329-2121 or visit chmuseums.org.

A few miles south of York on Highway 1, visit ***Brattonville.*** This is a restored village of 18th- and 19th-century structures erected by several gen-erations of the Bratton family. The homes are furnished with many Bratton pieces, including such items as an old-time biscuit press and a tin bath. One of the structures is a replica of a 1750 dirt-floored backwoodsman's cabin, complete with furniture and kitchen utensils. Other Bratton family structures include the Colonel William Bratton House from the 1760s, the Homestead from the 1820s, and Hightower Hall from the 1850s. A slave house, kitchen house, and dairy replicate typical outbuildings that would have been here. Call (803) 684-2327 or take a look at chmuseum.org for more historic back-ground. Admission is $6 for adults and $3 for students age 4 to 17.

Nearby ***Rock Hill*** is a relatively large town with a population of 67,000. Also settled by Scots and Irish, Rock Hill's name came from the hard rock the railroaders had to deal with when they were laying tracks. Perhaps the most prestigious attraction here is the beautifully designed and wonderfully situated *Winthrop University.* The lush campus, spread out under magnificent oaks and magnolias, is so pleasant you'll want to stroll into every corner of it. Be sure to do so—everybody does. While you stroll, note the *Little Chapel,* the building where the school started. Designed and built by America's first architect, Robert Mills, the Little Chapel originally was in Columbia. In 1936 it was moved here brick by brick. Mills later went on to Washington, DC, to design and help build the Washington Monument. There's more on Winthrop at winthrop.edu.

Rock Hill has a new formal entrance called *The Gateway,* which looks as if it should be guarding Lenin's tomb on Red Square or in storage at Universal Studios for use in an epic Roman movie. Two 60-foot Egyptian pillars and four 13-foot bronze statues have been artistically arranged around a circular plaza on David Lyles Boulevard—the effect is one of painful solemnity. New York sculptor Audrey Flack has created the four identical statues of muscular maidens, each holding aloft a symbol of Rock Hill's many accomplishments. According to the inscriptions on the statues' stone bases, the fire is symbolic of the flame of knowledge; the circle of stars represents the city's attention to culture; the set of gears symbolizes Rock Hill's business growth; and the bolt of lightning points out the role the production of electricity has had in Rock Hill's development. I parked here and read every word on every monument and came away convinced that this was the work of a very, very large committee. The kids will love it, but don't make them write a paper on it. There's much more on Rock Hill at cityofrockhill.com.

Paramount's *Carowinds* is a 100-acre water and theme park that straddles the North Carolina–South Carolina state line. Located on Carowinds Boulevard, Fort Mill, the park offers more than 40 state-of-the-art rides, shows, and movie-themed experiences for all ages. Just take I-77 to exit 90 at the North Carolina–South Carolina border. The park is just 15 minutes south of uptown Charlotte, North Carolina, and 12 miles north of Rock Hill, South Carolina. Thirty or so restaurants and snack stands provide a broad variety of dining choices, and the place is absolutely perfect for kids. They even have a gigantic wave pool. Call (803) 548-5300. Carowinds' website is carowinds.com, or you can write to 14523 Carowinds Blvd., Charlotte, NC 28273.

The Columbia Plateau

As you approach Columbia on I-77, the red clay rises slightly and begins to flatten out. Wildflowers, crepe myrtle, and even azaleas are planted in the median. And then you see it—the brand-new skyline with the copper dome of the old capitol building in the center. The city is on a wide, flat plateau that was once a plantation owned by one Mr. J. T. Taylor, who went public with the outcry: "They ruined a damn fine plantation and built a sorry-assed town." Probably the most scenic drive into the old city, over the great rivers that meet here, is from the west on Jarvis Klapman Boulevard—a name that doesn't exactly trip lightly over the tongue. Not too long ago we had a rash of avenues, bridges, landfills, and runoff culverts unfortunately named for politicians who were, and are, still in office. And since then a committee has actually named a wide, tree-lined, beautiful avenue Colonial Life Boulevard.

But there it is—**_Columbia._** Its gold and silver buildings and its copper dome stand under the reflecting clouds, illuminated like something out of a fairy tale or Disney World or the Land of Oz. The city is a study in contrasts. Out on the fringe you can still find combination general stores and service stations that sell night crawlers, bloodworms, and crickets to the anglers and candy from a curved glass case to the kids. You'll see smoked hams and mule collars along with fan belts and plow points hanging from the ceilings. Out front between the gas pumps will be the slick wooden bench where the old-timers still play checkers with bottle caps and watch the traffic going by.

Against these rustic reminders of the 1930s, the 1940s, and the 1950s, the city claims 15-story buildings of steel and colored glass, gourmet restaurants, three ballet companies, and a very fine South Carolina Shakespeare Company that performs for free in the city parks. The airport even offers nonstop air service to New York City and one-stop service to Los Angeles. And, just eight blocks west of the State House—in the center of the city— the Congaree River runs by the State Museum and Congaree Vista Park. It's right here in the Congaree that you can, with just a few arrangements, take a crack at catching a striped bass. The record was set fairly recently—48 pounds. This is something you won't find in too many cities out there in the great Republic.

When Kirk Finlay was mayor of Columbia, back in the 1970s, he had a vision. He thought that this part of the city, between the capitol and the

The South Carolina State Fair

Part of the joy of living here in the "hard lard belt" and celebrating surviving the summers is fall and the **South Carolina State Fair** in mid-October. It's the biggest extravaganza down here. There is nothing even close to it. For exact days, call (803) 799-3387 or visit scstatefair.org. A few of the contests are biscuit making from scratch, Rebel yells, clogging, chicken impersonations, hog steeplechases, and duck slides. And through it all are more lights, neon, and calliope and country music than the average person can stand. One wag calls the country music "ignorance set to music." If you decide to go, take my advice and lose a few pounds before you set foot on the premises, because every red-blooded church in town has a food booth and everything is knock-down delicious.

Last year, for no apparent reason, I drifted over to the Hog Show and asked a few questions that I'd been saving up for a few years. The big one was how the judges pick a champion hog. The judge I cornered told me more than I wanted to know; this man had all the facts. "Friend, we judge hogs on one point and one point only: how much meat that fellow can deliver. If there's one extra pork chop on that hog, I don't care if he's got one eye and four ears, that hog is our number one. Friend, raising hogs is a business, this ain't no kennel club." He kept calling me friend. "Friend, you got to figure the less overall fat, the more hog you'll get for your money. Now take a fat, wide fellow with a lot of extra jowl hanging down. That hog ain't good for nothing. And I mean nothing, in my estimation, turns a judge off faster than a hog that can't walk."

I asked him why, if everything was so slide-ruled out for the butcher counter, the owners hot-combed and powdered the hogs before showing. "Well friend, it's the exact same reason a girl will primp in front of a mirror. Showmanship! They want that hog to step out there with the best possible chance." He handed me a tract and a bumper sticker, HOGS ARE BEAUTIFUL. "We're out to improve the image of the hog and maybe bring a little of that beef money down to us. Lot of people figure hogs are dirty and will eat anything you put in front of them. Friend, you give a hog a chance and he'll live a lot cleaner than most people." So much for hogs.

river, held great promise as a way to revitalize downtown Columbia. It was mostly made up of small warehouses, and it was anchored by an old building that was the former printing operation for the Confederacy. There was just one problem, and it was not a small one. Railroad tracks ran right through the middle of that part of town, and not only was it an eyesore, but it also tied up traffic about four times a day. But Kirk had a plan. He got a big grant plus some state money, and he buried the railroad tracks in a tunnel. It worked like white on rice. Developers began pouring money in and, lo and behold, the Confederate Printing Plant became a Publix; some hotels, shops, galleries, and fine restaurants began to sprout; and today *The Congaree Vista,* as it is now known, rocks.

Columbia is also the home of the *University of South Carolina* (founded in 1801), which has grown from an enrollment of 4,000 students in the 1950s to a present-day student body of more than 31,000 at the campus in the heart of town. USC has a medical school and a law school, and for the past few years, the USC School of International Business has been rated among the nation's best by *U.S. News and World Report.* See a good profile of USC at sc.edu/aboutusc.

The city prides itself on the state-of-the-art *Richland Library* at 1431 Assembly St., an architectural masterpiece on four levels, each approximately one acre. This more than 242,000-square-foot building is one of the largest for an urban community of its size in the Southeast. The beautiful steel and glass construction with wonderful natural lighting and a forest of trees is truly all a library should be. The centerpiece here is the permanent art on the Garden Library, a 40-foot mural 18 feet high depicting the "wild rumpus scene" and two freestanding characters, all from Maurice Sendak's children's classic *Where the Wild Things Are.* This is the first time Sendak has authorized such use of his work as public art. The work is not only a wonderful background for the children's area but has also been designed and painted to allow the children to touch it. If you're traveling with kids, put the library on the top of your list. Call (803) 799-9084 or visit richlandlibrary.com/main.

The city also has numerous theaters and theater groups, an enormous and beautiful inner-city park, the very successful *South Carolina Philharmonic,* and the very fine *Columbia Museum of Art.* Located in the center of town at 1515 Main St., the museum offers one of the better permanent collections of Renaissance, Baroque, and Impressionist art in the entire Southeast. Among the artists represented are Botticelli, Canaletto, Tintoretto, Monet, Matisse, Renoir, and such regional artists as Elizabeth O'Neill Verner from Charleston and Jasper Johns, who is from the Columbia area. The museum is open Tues through Fri from 11 a.m. to 5 p.m., Sat from 10 a.m. to 5 p.m., and Sun from noon to 5 p.m. On the first Fri of the month the museum is open until 8 p.m. Closed on Mon. Admission is $10 for adults,

$8 for senior citizens, and $5 for students; children age 5 and under get in free. Sun admission is free for everyone. Call (803) 799-2810 or learn more at columbiamuseum.org.

A performance venue on the USC campus in the heart of the city is the **Koger Center,** a remarkable 2,254-seat auditorium with one of the best stages in the country. It's located at 1051 Greene St. See what's happening there at koger.sc.edu or call (803) 777-7500.

Getting into and out of downtown Columbia was made driver-friendly with the completion of a beltway around the entire city that connects three interstates and joins Columbia—via I-77, I-26, and I-20—to Charleston, Greenville, and Charlotte, North Carolina. Only 11 other cities in the nation share this style of highway transportation system. Now you can drive non-stop from Cleveland all the way to Charleston.

Thirty years ago the only ethnic food you could get in the old Columbia was pizza or maybe a Greek salad. Now, owing to the university's growing number of Asian students and the cosmopolitan population of the army stationed nearby at Fort Jackson, every cuisine from Vietnamese to Turkish to Indian to take-out sushi is available here. The schools have been integrated since the 1960s and are working as smoothly as those anywhere in the United States—they may, in fact, be better than most. And, at a time when whites-only country clubs are still flourishing across the nation, five of Columbia's six clubs are integrated.

Another stop should be the **South Carolina State Museum** at 301 Gervais St. The building is an old cotton mill, and the floors are foot-thick maple, which was needed to support the heavy textile machinery. This state-of-the-art museum has marvelous exhibits about natural history, science, and technology, with hands-on displays for kids. They can light up a laser beam, talk into the whisper dish and hear their voices across the room, and even handle the fossilized teeth of an extinct mastodon. The transportation display has an ancient 1904 Oldsmobile as well as a modern space suit worn by General Charles M. Duke Jr., an astronaut from South Carolina. Open Mon through Sat from 10 a.m. to 5 p.m. and Sun from 1 to 5 p.m. Adults pay $7 and children age 3 to 12 pay $5; free for children age 2 and under. Call (803) 898-4921 or visit museum.state.sc.us.

The South's largest children's museum and the best in America is **EdVenture** at 211 Gervais St. Walk into EdVenture, and the first thing you'll see is a giant 40-foot statue of a boy ("The World's Largest Child") sitting cross-legged, wearing a baseball cap, with kids crawling all over and inside him. His watch is an actual clock for the museum (although upside down!). His insides are a McDonald's Play Place–type sliding/climbing structure. But there's more. Go into his heart area and hear the beating pulse; the stomach rumbles and grumbles; and the brain's synapses snap, crackle, and pop, totally delighting those who have made it to the top. And this is just the beginning of the adventure at EdVenture. There's the farm room, complete with a milking cow, chickens that lay eggs, real tractors, and more. Cross over to the next room to climb into a real fire engine (put on some fire gear, too). Interested in being a sheriff or a builder? Want to change a real tire on a car? The tools are everywhere. Over to the other side of the building, as well as upstairs and outside, you'll find an Australian room (teaching you all sorts of Outback magic); a giant spider web in which to crawl around; a critter garden; a computer room; a dentist's office, where you can extract teeth; and the list just runs on and on.

Admission is $11.50; it's free for babies under a year of age. Save money by purchasing a yearlong pass, because you will use it! The museum is open from 9 a.m. to 5 p.m. Tues through Sat and noon to 5 p.m. Sun. For more information go to edventure.org or call (803) 779-3100.

On up Gervais another block is **_Longhorn Steakhouse,_** at 902A Gervais St., which advertises "no quiche, no ferns." Instead they have country music, enough neon for a state fair, and the best steaks in town with a very good salad for a modest price. This is a big place with many tables and booths. The service is excellent, and the prices are around $20. Call (803) 254-5100. For the other area Longhorn locations, see longhornsteak house.com.

One of the best but only slightly off-the-beaten path restaurants in the Vista Alley area is **_Motor Supply Company_** at 920 Gervais St. Years ago the building that now houses the restaurant was an auto-parts warehouse and store. When the management of the restaurant bought and began renovating the building, they found the old motor supply sign in the basement. It proved so irresistible that not only was the name used, but the sign itself now hangs over the main door. Of special interest on the inside is an enormous oak back bar with marble columns that look as if they came out of a Roman bath.

This upscale restaurant features chicken, lamb, veal, steak, seafood, and a variety of pasta dishes and is locally famous for its desserts. They also have a wide range of very good wines. Prices are around $12 for lunch and range from $20 to $28 for dinner. Open for lunch Tues through Sat from 11:30 a.m. to 2:30 p.m. Dinner is served from 5:30 to 9:30 p.m. Tues through Thurs, 5:30 to 10:30 p.m. Fri and Sat, and 5:30 to 9 p.m. Sun. Closed Mon. Sunday brunch is served from 10:30 a.m. to 2:30 p.m. Call (803) 256-6687 for reservations or just drop in. Their website is motorsupplycobistro.com.

While writing this book, I've used the word *best* only a couple of times. Well, here's one more, but this one would be a mortal sin to leave out—the *best* desserts in Columbia. *Nonnab's* restaurant at 930 Gervais St. in the Vista has been voted the favorite dessert spot in town for 14 years in a row. Serving a light fare of sandwiches, salads, and crepes for lunch Mon through Fri from 11:30 a.m. to 2 p.m. and quesadillas, pastas, seafood, and a petit filet for dinner, the real reason to come here is their frothy cappuccinos and large selection of cakes, pies, cheesecakes, and tarts for dessert. They are open for dinner Mon through Thurs from 5 to 11 p.m. On Fridays they open at 5 p.m. until 12:30 a.m. and on Saturdays opening a bit later at 6 p.m. and closing at 12:30 a.m. So this is the perfect stop after the theater or a concert. And if your sweet tooth needs some attention early in the day, they have now opened *The Pastry Shop at Nonnab's* right next door. This bakeshop will get your mouth watering for their breads, muffins, scones, brownies, and artisan pastries. The Pastry Shop is open from 7 a.m. to 2 p.m. Mon through Fri. Call (803) 779-9599 or go to nonnahs.com.

A block west of Nonnah's at 804 Gervais St. is *Adlub Milling Company,* which produces flour, meals, corn-bread mix, and another dozen milled products. Their old red neon has been burning high on the roof over Columbia for as long as most people can remember. Adluh is owned by the Allen brothers, who have made a career out of supporting education in the state through donations and scholarships to colleges and universities. The factory itself offers guided tours for schoolchildren, Scouts, senior citizens, and other groups. Each tour is capped with a visit to their hospitality room, where biscuits or hush puppies are baked right before your eyes, from the flour you just saw made, and served with butter, jams, and jellies. If you'd like to get on one of these tours, which will take you through the mill and show you how flour and the various milled products are made, one of the staff will try to join you up with a group. Call (803) 779-2460. Visit adluh store.com or phone (800) 692-3584 to place your order.

A few blocks from Adluh Flour is *Miyo's* at 922 S. Main St. This is a very fine restaurant specializing in Shanghai and Szechuan cuisine, located right in the center of the city. Michelle and Yong Wang, both from New York City, moved here a few years ago and have quickly catapulted into the absolute top spot in the entire county for Chinese cooking. They have a beautiful mahogany bar where they serve warm and chilled sake, liquor, and fine wines. They have remodeled and refurnished the old building so that now, along with the delicious food, you can sit in a stunning setting of Asian art. Hours are Mon through Fri from 11:30 a.m. to 10 p.m. and Sat from 4:30 to 10 p.m. Prices are around $10 for lunch, $15 to $25 for dinner. You can also call ahead for take-out service. Call (803) 779-6496 or visit miyos .com to see their extensive menu and other locations.

The Oyster Bar at 1123 Park St., in the heart of the Vista, is precisely that: an oyster bar. There are no ferns, no side dishes, no sauces, no beds of lettuce and pasta, not even a garnish. Condiments, soup, and crackers are the only edibles on the table. Your waiter shucks your oysters and brings you drinks, and that's the way it's supposed to be. Oysters are $11.50 for a dozen. If you prefer steamed shrimp or scallops, they are priced at $19 and $22 a pound. Very friendly place, and if you go there, you'll be back. Call (803) 799-4484 or see oysterbarcolumbia.com. Hours are 4 to 11 p.m. Mon through Sat.

You can't miss the *State House* on the corner of Main and Gervais; it's in the center of everything. This blue granite building was shelled by Sherman in 1865 from across the Congaree River. The spots where the shells landed are marked on the western side of the building with bronze stars. On the steps of the capitol is a bronze statue of George Washington, with his cane broken off. The story and the inscription tell us the Union forces "brickbatted it." Open Mon through Fri 9 a.m. to 5 p.m. You can go inside and take the free tour conducted from 9 a.m. to noon and from 1:30 to 3:30 p.m. Call (803) 734-2430 or visit scstatehouse.gov.

A block south at 1012 Sumter St., just behind the State House, is the *Town Theatre.* While the building dates from 1924, the theater has the distinguished record of running continuously for more than 90 years. The actors, directors, and stagehands are all local citizens. Call (803) 799-2510 for current schedules or check out towntheatre.com.

The *Trustus Theater* at 520 Lady St. is another interesting theater, providing deep comfortable couches as well as soft drinks, beer, and popcorn for the audiences. First-class entertainment and professionally acted and staged plays are always on the playbill here. Call (803) 254-9732 for their current schedule. The website is trustus.org.

notsofast!

One night back in the 1960s, Satchel Paige, the famous baseball pitcher, was stopped by the police in the middle of Gervais Street for speeding. When the police recognized him, and after he gave them a stack of autographed 8-by-11s for their friends and families, they formed a motorcade around his big Cadillac and escorted him on across and out onto the highway to Atlanta.

Two blocks north of the capitol is the *Equitable Arcade Building* at 1332 Main St. This amazing and beautiful structure, built in Second Renaissance Revival style in 1912, was Columbia's first enclosed shopping mall. It is now on the National Register of Historic Places. Shaped like an L with ornamental facades both on Main Street and around the corner on Washington Street, the two-story Arcade has a central hallway lighted by an enormous skylight. The facing is white terra-cotta marble and decorated ceramic tile. Six huge double-tiered bronze chandeliers provide evening lighting. With all the glass and light and white marble, the old building looks not unlike the gallerias of Florence or Venice. It's a downtown tragedy that the building, probably the most delicate, attractive, and unique structure in the entire city, hasn't been renovated and put to better use. In any event, stop by and walk through. You'll never see anything quite like it again.

Just up Main a couple more blocks is the recently relocated *Nickelodeon,* South Carolina's nonprofit cinema. They have been screening foreign and independent films in Columbia since 1979. The "Nick" has a loyal following and moved to the old Fox Theatre location at 1607 Main St. amidst much fanfare and celebration in the fall of 2012. The renovated 99-seat theater is run by the Columbia Film Society and shows over 100 films, 362 days a year. Together with *Mast General Store* next door, they are ushering in a revitalization of the Main Street corridor for downtown Columbia.

Call (803) 254-3433 or check their website, nickelodeon.org, for upcoming events and showtimes.

On the corner of Richland and Pickens is the **Seibels House,** the oldest house in Columbia. Built in 1796, it is surrounded by palmetto trees. A separate kitchen built of handmade bricks stands behind the house, and there's a large and beautiful garden at the side. Today the house is the administrative headquarters of the **Historic Columbia Foundation.** They're located at 1601 Richland St.; call (803) 252-7742. Their helpful website is historic columbia.org.

Within walking distance from the Seibels House is the impressive **Robert Mills House and Gardens** at 1616 Blanding St. Robert Mills is the architect who designed the Washington Monument in our nation's capital, among other important landmarks in Columbia and around South Carolina. Across the street at 1615 Blanding is the **Hampton-Preston Mansion and Gardens,** home of the Wade Hampton family. The first Wade Hampton served in the Revolutionary War and was a general in the War of 1812; Wade Hampton II was an officer in the War of 1812; and Wade Hampton III commanded the Confederate cavalry during the Civil War and later became governor of South Carolina.

The Mann-Simons Site, at 1403 Richland St., was the home of Celia Mann, a slave from Charleston who purchased her freedom with money she earned as a midwife. She walked to Columbia, bought this property, and made her home here until her death years later. Today on the ground floor of the cottage, the only remaining structure of a collection of buildings owned by her family until 1970, is an exhibit telling the story of Celia Mann and her entrepreneurial descendants, the restoration of the cottage, and ongoing archaeological explorations on-site.

The Woodrow Wilson Family Home, at 1705 Hampton St., is another museum house presented by Historic Columbia Foundation and the only presidential historic site in South Carolina. However, an extensive restoration program is currently under way, which will keep this site closed for the immediate future except for special tours offered from time to time to showcase the progress being made. Still, this is a fascinating place to see—if only from the outside, which has been beautifully repainted in appropriate Victorian colors. When done, the boyhood home of "Tommy" Woodrow Wilson will display many Wilson family pieces, including the bed in which

Woodrow Wilson was born. Wilson's father, Joseph Ruggles Wilson, was a Presbyterian minister; he and his wife are buried only a few blocks away at Columbia's First Presbyterian Church, where Reverend Wilson served.

Tickets for all the house museums under the auspices of the Historic Columbia Foundation are sold in the Museum Shop on the ground floor of the Robert Mills House. Tour tickets are $6 per house for adults and $5 for college students, seniors 65 or older, and active-duty military personnel. For ages 6 through 17, the cost is $3; for younger than age 6, it's free. Hours are 10 a.m. to 4 p.m. Tues through Sat (last tour at 3 p.m.) and 1 to 5 p.m. Sun (last tour at 4 p.m.). A combination ticket for the Robert Mills, Hampton-Preston, and Mann-Simons houses is offered as well.

Another two-dozen historic sites in Columbia are worth seeing. Among the most notable are **Tapp's Department Store** (now **Tapp's Art Center**) at 1644 Main St., **Sylvan's Jewelry** at 1500 Main St., the **South Carolina Governor's Mansion** at 800 Richland St., and the **Lace House** directly across from it.

Modeled on the open-pit design of the San Diego Zoo, **Riverbanks Zoo and Garden** is rated one of the top 10 zoos in the country year after year. Its budget is more than $4 million a year, and it houses more than 2,000 animals in natural settings without cages. In addition, more than 1,000 reptiles, amphibians, and fish from around the world are housed in an aquarium-reptile complex. Located at 500 Wildlife Pkwy., the Saluda River runs between the zoo and the botanical gardens, and the anglers who hear the animal calls at night or in the early morning say it's like being on the Amazon. Kids love the huge seal and sea lion pool, especially at feeding time. Very good outdoor snack bars serve almost anything you like for lunch.

If you're one of those people who is going to drive from Cleveland to Charleston on the interstates, and you can only make one stop in Columbia, I'd make it the zoo. You can't go wrong: Recently the zoo has expanded its facilities and is now housing four gorillas, four koala bears, and an elaborate bird exhibit where you purchase nectar for $2 and South American birds will drink it right out of your hand. Kids love it. Be sure to bring your camera along because the shots of the kids feeding the birds are wonderful. Very safe for all ages. Open daily 9 a.m. to 5 p.m. (until 6 p.m. on Sat and Sun Apr through Sept). Admission is $11.75 for adults (age 13 and over) and $9.25

for children age 3 to 12; children 2 and under admitted free. For further information call (803) 779-8717 or visit riverbanks.org.

Back on Main Street, a little surprise in Columbia for breakfast and lunch is *Cafe 1201.* It's on the mezzanine level of the Capitol Center Building at 1201 Main St., overlooking the State House grounds. Early every morning they begin baking their fine bread products, cleaning their produce for salads and sandwiches, preparing their soups, and grinding their coffee beans. Breakfast is served weekdays starting at 7:30 a.m. and lunch runs until 3 p.m. On their menu you will find assorted muffins and cakes (including a daily cake special), and even homemade foccacia. Their hot hero sandwiches are some of the best around, and you gotta love a cafe that offers a fried bologna and cheese. If you like, you can walk it down the street to the fountain or sit out front under the big tree with the paper and watch the passing parade. Very pleasant. Very good. Their tantalizing bakery items are also available at the *All Local Farmers' Market* on Saturday mornings at 711 Whaley St. Call (803) 255-6292 for more information.

Hampton Street Vineyard is a lovely restaurant at 1201 Hampton St. in downtown Columbia, catering to those who enjoy fine dining, fine wining, and a relaxing time. *Wine Spectator* magazine gave it the prestigious "Best Award of Excellence," and there's a reason why: With over 650 different types of wines in stock, they're able to offer 35 wines by the glass! Unprecedented in our neck of the woods, and the food is simply delicious. Lunch is served Mon through Fri 11:30 a.m. to 2 p.m., dinner Mon through Sat 6 to 10 p.m. The bar opens at 5 p.m. Mon through Sat. Call (803) 252-0850. Their whole menu is online at hamptonstreetvineyard.com.

Nestled directly behind the Adam's Mark Hotel in the heart of the heart of Columbia at 1230 Hampton St., where it has been for many years, is Columbia's premier lunchtime spot: *The Hampton Place Cafe.* Not fancy but great! Specializing in gourmet sandwiches, homemade crab and spinach-mushroom quiches, and Greek and Caesar salads, owner Steve Gendel packs them in every day for lunch. The average price with drink is around $9. His only advice is that you get there early to get a seat. Open Mon through Fri 10:30 a.m. to 4 p.m. Call (803) 254-5847 or check it out at hamptonplacecafe.com.

Hampton Place is a great spot to use as a center for seeing the new downtown Columbia. One block away is the wonderfully set up *Columbia*

Museum of Art, Main and Hampton Streets, which houses a truly fabulous permanent collection. Call (803) 799-2810 or visit columbiamuseum.org.

Across the street from the museum is ***Cowboy Brazilian Steakhouse,*** 1508 Main St. (803-728-0887 or cowboybraziliansteakhouse.com), a *churrascaria* serving a series of 16 different meats on skewers carved at your table by a parade of gauchos. Be sure you are hungry when you go, because they also have a 25-item salad bar with hot Brazilian side dishes. And the South American wines and *caipirinha* complete the Brazilian steak house experience. The building is a marvelous renovation of the Art Deco Kress Dime Store from the 1930s. Almost all decorations have been preserved, as well as the entire front facade, which is covered with gold leaf. It's a masterpiece of renovation and a brilliant landmark in Columbia's new downtown recovery. From the Brazilian Steakhouse, you can stroll three blocks down Main to the State House and the surrounding parks.

Who could resist trying a restaurant where the head cook is named "Chef Fatback"? I mean, come on, you know you want to try it. ***Mac's on Main,*** 1710 Main St. (803-929-0037 or macsjazznblues.com), serves up—need I say it?—an all-you-can-eat lunch buffet of ribs, fried catfish, Cajun pork chops, and meat loaf. Viola's macaroni and cheese and Mac's peach cobbler walk and talk Southern comfort food. Dinner is served starting at 6 p.m., and live jazz and blues bands play most nights. If you want to go local, you need to check this place out. The lunch buffet runs from 11 a.m. to 3 p.m. weekdays, and dinner goes until midnight or later on weekends. They are closed on Sun.

One more barbecue stop, for those of you who just can't get enough. ***Palmetto Pig*** at 530 Devine St. is a good downtown option if you have barbecue on your mind. The place is small and parking can be tight, so try to time your stop early or late to beat the buffet lineup. You have a choice of pulled pork barbecue or fried or barbecued chicken with sides of potato salad, hash, rice, corn, slaw, green beans, and baked beans. And in case that isn't enough, finish with banana pudding. Everything here is first-rate, cooked on the premises, and the value is good. University students and downtown workers, both blue- and white-collar types, share tables here, all knowing a good thing when they find it. It's open Tues and Wed for lunch from 11 a.m. to 2:30 p.m. and Thurs through Sat for lunch and dinner from 11 a.m. to 9 p.m. Excellent for takeout and large catered affairs. Call (803) 733-2556 or see palmettopig.com.

If you've got a craving for a little Tex-Mex, stop in *Tios Mexican Cafe & Cantina* at 921 Sumter St. downtown. This is a family-owned place, as in two brothers and three sisters, with really fresh homemade food. Try one of their regular daily specials; my personal favorite is the Wet Burrito (on Wed and Sun), which comes in a choice of five different versions. The Classic is a 12-inch flour tortilla stuffed with beans, cheese, tomatoes, and onions with enchilada sauce and either shredded chicken, ground chuck, or pulled pork. Be prepared to loosen your belt if you finish this one. They make four terrific salsas—the extra hot even won a national competition. They also have daily happy hour specials like sangria and margarita nights from 4 p.m. until closing. Tios has a fun atmosphere, and if you want to kick it up a notch or two, pick out a hot sauce from the extensive collection lining the walls. Spontaneous Combustion or King of Fire should get your mouth going, and if it doesn't, there's something wrong with you. To find out more, call them at (803) 252-7229 or visit tiossc.com. Delivery and catering are available, too.

Got the munchies? Swing in *Cromer's* on Huger Street and pick up some gourmet peanuts, handmade popcorn, classic candy, or caramel and candy apples. Their peanuts are "guaranteed the worst in town"—that's right—their slogan may be working a little reverse psychology on us. But they've been around since 1935, so they must be doing something right. Build a tin of your favorites—maybe some cheese, caramel, and buttered popcorn—or pick up the variety gift box with peanut brittle, cashews, pistachios, and popcorn. The combinations are endless. Some of their candies are bound to bring back a few memories. Who didn't love a mouthful of Double Bubble or Atomic Fireballs when we were kids? You'll see their sign at 1700 Huger St. Turn in and load up the car for your travels, or take some home to the family if you can resist tapping into the tin. Don't worry if you do, though, because you can always call them to ship some more at (800) 322-7688 or order online at cromers.com.

Sandy's Famous Hot Dogs, 825 Main St. (803-254-6914), is at the corner of College and Main Streets on the USC campus. This is about as down-home as it gets down here, and the prices will leave you standing there with your mouth open. Last time I was there, a grilled cheese sandwich was $3.19, and a very fine barbecue sandwich was $4.99. The Angus beef hot dogs are the signature and only $2.49, or $3.09 for a slaw dog. They make their own chili, slaw, and pimento cheese and are happy to top your dog with your favorite combinations. Don't leave the place without sampling at least one of their 32 flavors of ice cream, or go for it and get a banana split. Visit sandyshotdogs.com to find their other locations around town and to print a coupon for an even better deal.

Sandy's caters to a lot of construction workers around town who love them, as well as the crews who work down the road at the quarry several blocks away. From Sandy's take Main Street south to Whaley, and go west on Whaley Street until you hit Williams Street. Turn left here and ease down to the end, where you will be in the heart of the **Vulcan Rock Quarry.** This is a one-of-a-kind phenomenon that everyone should see. Basically it's an old rock quarry where they have been digging out granite for over 100 years. The heavy-duty trucks at the bottom will look like toys. The quarry, from where the granite is removed, is about a half-mile wide and 500 feet deep and is made up of 50-foot shelves staggered down the face of the pit. The breeze from the Congaree River only a few hundred yards away comes over the ridge and into the pit to create a vortex. While you can't see it, the buzzards, who have made a happy home here, can. Since they aren't too energetic to begin with, they love to sail around and around on the rising currents. You might see 8 or 10 at a time sailing along in their typical loose buzzard formation. Red-tailed hawks and eagles can also be spotted, and in the evening owls and red and gray foxes. This is a fascinating spectacle, and it's right in the center of town. Contact them at 545 Georgia St., (803) 771-0090, for visiting hours and tours Mon through Fri. There's more on Vulcan's quarry operations at vulcanmaterials.com.

Five Points, a mile or so southeast of the capitol, is the city's main center of activity. Here the university students gather to pound their drums and string their beads. At 2007 Devine, right in the heart of Five Points, is **Portfolio Art Gallery.** This is a small but packed-to-the-ceiling store that carries a huge variety of paintings, sculptures, blown-glass pieces, jewelry, and clay, wood, and paper pieces. Judith Roberts, who taught art in the local public school and is the owner, won national notice a few years back when she worked with a group of special-needs students, whose ages ranged from preschool to 21 years, on a huge 10-by-12-foot mural of animals and shrubs. Not only did it win the state competition, but it was eventually displayed at the Kennedy Center in Washington, DC.

Judith says, "I'm really not a terrific salesperson but I get excited talking about art, and I feel that most people like to talk about the paintings that interest them. They like to know something about the artist and why they respond favorably to his or her work. That's what I talk to them about—why a piece appeals to them—and I use basic compositional values in explaining its interest. Sometimes at midnight, I'll have 12 people in here. I've sold a painting at one in the morning." Hours are 10 a.m. to 6 p.m. Mon through Sat. Call (803) 256-2434 for more.

If you want to do Five Points right, you must eat at **Andy's Deli,** 2005 Greene St. Andy Shlon has run his family business (along with his two very handsome sons) since 1978, and he's never met a stranger. "Hello, my dear" and "Hello, my friend" are mainstays, as are the big, thick, unbeatable sandwiches and salads. (Andy's Special and the R2D2 are good enough to keep bringing you back and back.) We defy you to find any better place in this state. Even if you did find deli food to match, you'd not find it in combination with such a friendly atmosphere. Cash and checks only, but Andy's been known to tell regulars to bring the money back another time if they forget and flip out a credit card with no George Washingtons to be found. If you're looking to be a regular, this place is for you. We just like to call it home. Open from 10 a.m. to 9 p.m. Mon through Sat; closed Sun. Call (803) 799-ANDY.

The **Blue Cactus Cafe** in Five Points is definitely a must. Located at 2002H Greene St., the restaurant's decor is eclectic, with a sombrero hanging from the ceiling, a bookcase of hot sauces, postcards from customers from around the world, a world map with pins to show where customers are from, and a little display of snuff cans (very funky)—and this is just the beginning. Recommended lunch fare would be the *bee bim bob,* basically a bowl of rice with an assortment of Korean-style vegetables on top; your choice of beef, chicken, or tofu; and usually a fried egg served on top—you mix it all up. (Request what you want or don't want on it!) For dinner, try the curry chicken stir-fry (the owner's own recipe). Dinner for two, with appetizers and drinks, will cost under $25. And don't forget the tasty appetizers: *kim bob* (Korean seaweed roll—all vegetable) or Korean dumplings (meat, cabbage, clear noodles). You can always top off your meal with a bowl of Japanese adzuki ice cream, green tea, or ginger ice cream.

The Blue Cactus is truly a family-run place: Lloyd and Mary Reese are the owners and chefs; Mary's sisters and sisters-in-law help out in the back; and a slew of cousins and children help run the place as well. Go early, because they tend to get packed (the food is excellent!) and, as Lloyd's daughter laughingly says, "We're horribly slow, but Dad would say 'arrogantly' slow!" On a scale of 5 stars or spoons or forks or whatever, the Blue Cactus would surely get 10 of everything! Call (803) 929-0782 or visit bluecactuscafe.com.

You'll find **Claussen's Inn** at 2003 Greene St. a unique, comfortable, and very attractive place to stay. The old brick building used to be a bakery, and you can still see the logo in the bricks at the front. Inside, many of the 28 rooms have 20-foot ceilings, and the loft suites have winding staircases. In 1995, when William Styron, Joe Heller, William Manchester, Paul Fussel, James Dickey, Mickey Spillane, and Al Wertheim were in Columbia for a conference, they all stayed here. Rates range from $150 to $210, with a continental breakfast and refreshments in the afternoon. Claussen's is four blocks from the university and 100 yards from the center of Five Points. Call (803) 765-0440. Their website is theinnatclaussens.com.

Down the hill about 100 yards from Claussen's is **Garibaldi's,** 2013 Greene St. This is a first-class restaurant with an excellent wine list, a menu that changes daily, superb food, and a very fine staff. My favorite dish is the apricot-smothered, baked-to-a-crisp flounder. The bar is comfortable for long waits, and you have a fine view of Five Points. Prices for dinner range from $10 to $30. Open for dinner Mon through Thurs from 5:30 to 10:30 p.m., Fri and Sat from 5:30 to 11 p.m., and Sun from 5:30 p.m. to 10 p.m. Call (803) 771-8888 or visit garibaldicolumbia.com.

Across the street and a little farther down the hill is **Yesterday's Restaurant and Tavern,** 2030 Devine St. Out front up on the roof is a cowboy sitting in a bathtub with his 10-gallon hat and his boots and spurs on, which is an indicator of the inside atmosphere. Two televisions serve the bar and the local sports fans and university students. The rest of the space has booths and tables, and during lunch they're packed. Here's an idea for you: Skip a couple meals and come here and order the chicken-fried steak. It's served with white gravy, any three vegetables you can name, and all the corn bread you can handle. It will not only stick to every rib you've ever had, but it's as close to delicious as anything you'll ever eat. Open Sun through Thurs from 11:30 a.m. to midnight, and Fri and Sat from 11:30 a.m. to 1 a.m. Call (803) 799-0196 or visit yesterdayssc.com.

Leaving Yesterday's by the side door, you are directly in front of **Goat-feathers** at 2017 Devine St., an excellent coffeehouse that serves a lot more than just coffee. You can get a whole meal here of soup and French bread, fresh bagels, or fresh croissants, and you can get almost any dessert ever created. Goatfeathers is unquestionably one of the best and liveliest bars in town. A round table in the middle of the room seats 10 and is loaded with magazines and newspapers. A few years back they installed a cigar bar with at least 40 varieties from all over the world. They also have a good supply of Batman Zippo lighters. Call them at (803) 799-2276.

Groucho's at 611 Harden St. (803-799-5708) has the definite flavor of a New York deli. The pastrami and corned beef are excellent, and the service is fast and courteous. Great rye bread here, along with their signature sandwiches and special sauces. This is a famous hangout for Carolina students that goes back a long, long time. Hours are 11 a.m. to 4 p.m. Mon through Sat, 11 a.m. to 3 p.m. Sun. Great take-out service. Check out their other locations in Columbia and around the state at grouchos.com.

Pawley's Front Porch at 827 Harden St. (803-771-8001) is a great place to keep in mind for wraps, tacos, soups, and especially their monster specialty burgers. If you're up to the challenge, try the 8-ounce burger topped with pulled pork, fried mac and cheese, and coleslaw with mustard BBQ sauce. You may have caught them on the Food Network's *Diners, Drive-Ins and Dives,* when host Guy Fieri explored all the unusual combinations they pile on their burgers. The restaurant also has a huge-screen TV for catching the game, outdoor seating right in the heart of Five Points, and a lively crowd of steady customers. I like to sit outside, eat, and drink a cold one here whenever I get the chance. Hours are Sun through Thurs 11:30 a.m. to 9:30 p.m., Fri and Sat from 11 a.m. to 11 p.m. Their website touts the evening's specials at pawleysfrontporch.com.

I guess at some point I have to pick what I think is the best of the best restaurants in the old town. It's not quite off the beaten path; as a matter of fact, it's right smack in the middle of Five Points. It's called **Saluda's,** named for the river that runs through the town. The address is 751 Saluda Ave. (803-799-9500). First of all, you have to climb 20 steps to get to it, but every single step is worth it because this has to be the best food and the best service in town. Second, it has the best view of Five Points, and the 20-foot fountain that is its centerpiece. Third, in the spring and summer Saluda's helps sponsor a Wednesday-evening music program, with big local and touring bands playing everything: jazz, rock, lite rock, bluegrass, and Broadway show tunes. Anyhow, when you're dining at Saluda's out on a beautiful terrace, you have the best seat in the house for the music, because you're literally looking down on it only 30 or 40 feet away.

Saluda's also has a private dining area that can host up to 50 people—ideal for bridal showers, business meetings, or any private party. Their main dining room can host up to 125 guests, depending on your seating arrangements. Along with an extensive wine list of over 300 selections, the chef here offers an eclectic mix of American and continental cuisine. One of the specials is the grilled sweet tea–brined pork chop with a barbecue glaze. Another is a black and white sesame seed–crusted fillet of salmon, pan-seared and served over wasabi mashed potatoes, with a side of seasonal vegetables. The menu changes seasonally. You can check their website, saludas.com, to see what's new on the menu. Hours are Mon through Sun 5 to 11 p.m. Good tip: Show up here some evening for a cool cocktail out on the patio overlooking the fountain. And while you're here, find out what days the orchestra is playing and make your reservations.

Someone once said that the South knows as much about cooking veal as a hog knows about the Lord's plan for salvation. I shall now lay that myth to rest. At **Dianne's on Devine,** 2400 Devine St., just up the hill from Five Points, they make a veal piccata that rivals anything in the five boroughs of New York. The very thin milk-fed veal is sautéed in a light egg batter with fresh herbs and finished with white wine, lemon, and capers. It is a joy and a wonder. The other veals crossing the finish line with colors flying are parmigiana, marsala, saltimbocca, Antoinette, and Fellini. The Caesar salad here is first rate, as is every one of the appetizers. A good suggestion is to have two appetizers, a salad, and a good bottle of wine. They also have air-conditioned patio dining. And don't forget to tell Dianne I sent you.

On occasional Wed nights at Dianne's, the popular Ross Holmes and his band play beach music, show tunes, and standards and will play anything you can name. He does a great job of singing "Summer Wind" and almost everything Sinatra ever recorded. Fri and Sat nights usually offer other live entertainment and jazz. The prices here range from $13 for pasta to $32 for dinner. There's a great bar, with interesting bartenders and a good supply of local characters. Try it, you can't go wrong. Hours for dining are Mon 5 to 9 p.m. and Tues through Sat 5 to 10 p.m. The phone is (803) 254-3535, and the website is diannesondevine.com.

Even though **Za's** is not considered a kids' restaurant, it's my kid's favorite Columbia hangout. She likes to take the dogs to lunch or dinner, stick their leashes on the patio chair, and order a pizza outside (the patio is a huge dining area in itself). She's been coming here since she was six months old, so she should know what's good—she orders the T-Zone, which is basically a sandwich pizza, served with either fresh fruit, chips, pasta salad, or coleslaw. Of course, everyone orders the fruit salad, because this is the sort of restaurant that serves really fresh fruit. Inside, the restaurant is attractive and big, without seeming to be too big—expect a good ambience, with low lighting, copper decor, and good-looking waitstaff. Sunday lunch is a good time to go, because it isn't too crowded. Weekends you'll have to wait—proof of how really good this restaurant is—and it's worth the wait. It's at 2930 Devine St. Hours are Mon through Wed 11 a.m. to 10 p.m., Thurs and Fri 11 a.m. to 11 p.m., Sat 11 a.m. to 10 p.m., and Sun 11 a.m. to 9 p.m. Learn more at zasbrickovenpizza.com or call (803) 771-7334.

Arabesque is the perfect restaurant if you are in the mood for some thoroughly scrumptious Middle Eastern fare that will fill up your stomach and leave your wallet full. The most expensive meal served is the baked kibbeh (an oven-baked blend of cracked wheat and ground beef, spices, and pine nuts served with a side of plain yogurt) for just under $10. Grape leaves, hummus, baba ghanouj (roasted eggplant blended with tahini), and kibbeh can be found in the appetizers or in the Arabesque Sampler, and these are so good you might just want to order everything two or three times and forget about an entree. Of course, it would be hard to turn down an entree such as a kabob, a shawarma, a tawouk, or a mujadara. If you don't know what these are, run, don't walk (no, drive!), as fast as you can and try them out. They're better tasted than described. Don't forget to top whatever it is you do eat with one of the fabulous under-$2 desserts. (We also highly recommend the cucumber and yogurt salad.) This is Middle Eastern food done just right! Arabesque is at 2930 Devine St. (803-779-6299), right next door to Za's.

Found in just about every major neighborhood in Columbia (we highly recommend the one on Beltline), *Lizard's Thicket* has turned into a capital institution. Those who are fans are either eating there now, are on their way to eat there, or have just finished eating there and are planning their next trip. Banana pudding is the ultimate dessert, and if you don't want to cook on a major holiday, they open their doors with holiday fare. This is fast, inexpensive, home-cooked food (but not "fast food"), with waitresses you'll want to adopt as aunts. The only downside of Lizard's Thicket is that they aren't in other parts of the United States—just another reason to come to South Carolina. (My sister-in-law makes annual trips down here from New York just so she can spend a week eating at Lizard's Thicket. She doesn't miss one meal—which makes it really easy on the wife.) Call (803) 738-0006 or check out their 14 locations at lizardsthicket.com.

McAlister's Deli has four places: one at 4710 Forest Dr. (803-790-5995); one at 300 Columbiana Dr. (803-781-4550); one at 119 Sparkleberry Ln. (803-788-7600); and one more at 5175 Sunset Blvd. in Lexington (803-951-3332). All are excellent and have fine service and a wonderful menu of deli sandwiches, salads, soups, and desserts. Very good corned beef and pastrami sandwiches, as well as excellent soups in a bread bowl, if you like. Very good lemonade, too, and they are known for their sweet tea, a Southern staple. A money-saving "just for kids" menu is also available. Hours are 10:30 a.m. to 10 p.m. seven days a week. Find out more at mcalistersdeli.com.

Lillian's at 4711 Forest Dr. is the place in Columbia to have lunch if you're in the mood for a tea party. Not that they really focus on tea, because they do not, or that you have to dress up, because you don't—but the ambience of a grown-up tea party is there. Try the turkey and cucumber sandwiches, or the vegetarian wraps, or the lemon squares, or anything. It's all delicious and homemade. Open only for lunch, Mon through Fri from 10 a.m. to 4 p.m. and Sat from 10 a.m. to 3 p.m.; credit cards accepted only for orders of $25 or more. Call (803) 790-0733.

Don't expect to move much when you leave the table at *The Original Pancake House* at 4840 Forest Dr. Pancakes come with everything, and they're so tasty you can't help eating them—all. The focus is on pancakes, but the crepes will make your teeth ache, they're so good. Be careful ordering the omelette: It's about the size of a football, and you'll be forced to eat the whole thing because it is a scientifically proven fact that a person can't stop until the last bite. In fact, everything is served fast (except on Sunday, when the church crowd hits), but expect to waddle out slowly—and satisfied. Call (803) 782-6742 or visit originalpancakehouse.com.

About a mile south of the capitol, the **Rosewood Market and Deli,** at 2803 Rosewood Dr., is a one-of-a-kind success story for natural and organic foods. The deli operates seven days a week and features hot meals twice daily. Much of the food here has a macrobiotic slant, but some dairy and fish are occasionally used. On any given day you can find local and international artists happily spooning up their tofu on the outside patio. Call (803) 765-1083 or visit rosewoodmarket.com.

Casey's Fireworks at 3830 Rosewood has probably the wildest mix of products you'll see on the East Coast. They're the biggest seller of fireworks in the state. If you're lucky enough to run into John Casey, he'll give you an education about the fireworks industry. Basically the Japanese, who have had some recovery in their economy during the past 50 years, have stopped making fireworks. The reason is there were too many explosions and too many casualties. An example John cites is Roman candles. He says in order to produce a good Roman candle, you have to pack the powder down as tight as possible. But the catch is, if you pack it too tight, it blows up. Nowadays most of the Roman candles are produced in China.

Another trend in fireworks is the drop in popularity in the old macho exploders; i.e., torpedoes, cherry bombs, 6-inch-long firecrackers, etc. Today women, who are doing most of the buying, are insisting on more safety and more colors. The big sellers are now sparklers, fountains, sprays, and much more colorful exploding rockets. A few of the newer Chinese products are the Celestial Spider, Mammoth Chrysanthemum, Golden Spider, Crackling Delight, Blinking Dragon's Breath, and Fountain with Thunderclaps. Casey's doesn't increase their prices for any holiday and go out of their way to teach safe handling and practices. Call them at (803) 738-9173 or visit caseysfire works.com.

Maybe fireworks aren't your thing. Maybe golf is. If so, a little practice with the sticks is always good for the soul. The **Columbia East Driving Range** is 3 miles past the Veterans' Hospital on Garner's Gerry Road and is directly across from an open-air produce market, which sells everything from watermelons and okra to hot boiled peanuts. Over the years this range has attracted a group of regulars who look and act not unlike the cast of *Cheers,* but with more political savvy and much better material.

But it's not all fun and games out at Columbia East. It's all business on the driving range, which is lighted for as far as the eye can see and stays open until the last person stops swinging. Inside, they have an array of new and used clubs, and if you like, they can assemble almost anything you want, including stock heads, shafts, and grips. They also have golf caps, bags, gloves, and umbrellas. In short, if you play the game, this is where you can get everything at an affordable price. As for balls, this is the place to go to save some serious money. Slightly used Titleists, which normally cross the counter when new at $3 a pop, are only two for a dollar, and you won't be able to find a blemish or a scratch. Sound advice: Load up on these as well as Maxflis, Wilsons, etc. They also sells Vienna sausage, pickled eggs, hot dogs, fruit cakes, dill pickles, beer, soft drinks, and small-bore candies and mints. You'll find Columbia East at 8041 Garner's Ferry Rd. Call (803) 695-1220.

Fifteen or so miles out Highway 378, almost to Sumter, is the sprawling ***Mr. Bunky's Restaurant and Market*** at 10441 Garner's Ferry Rd., Eastover (803-783-3501). As they say in the trade, "Here you will find anything." For once it's true. Name it and it's here. From horse saddles to crickets and worms to fresh baked goods. From cook stoves, shovels, and rakes to boiled peanuts, fresh meat, and produce: local watermelons, grapes, strawberries, peaches, and cantaloupes. On one wing there's a full-size buffet restaurant that serves three meals a day, and on the second floor out behind the homemade rocking chairs and bird houses sits a white cockatoo called "Mr. Sunshine." The kids love him and crowd around while he preens and tells them what's going on in the bird world. If you like fishing and forgot your tackle, you can get everything you can possibly need for fly casting, bait casting, pole fishing, or even frog gigging. Mr. Bunky, or one of his relatives, will be glad to give you all the information you need about where to go and what to use for bait.

If you are in Columbia on a Friday or Saturday night, a spot you shouldn't miss is ***Bill's Music Shop and Pickin' Parlor*** at 710 Meeting St., West Columbia. Some of the best bluegrass groups in the country play here and, after they decide they like it, sometimes stay for four and five weeks. The Open Stage starts at 7:30 p.m. (doors open at 6 p.m.) followed

Ode to the Capitol

If there was such a place as the exact center of Columbia, and maybe even all of South Carolina, where the wires, the politics, and the liaisons all came together, the **Capitol Restaurant** was it, and it was that way for 50 or so years. If you started with your back facing the statue of the Confederate soldier in front of the steps of the capitol and walked up Main Street for half a block, you'd see the old and fading green awning of the Capitol.

It all happened on Tuesday nights while the legislature was in session—from the second Tuesday in January to the end of the first week in June. The house band on these Tuesdays included Commissioner Rudolph Mitchell on keyboard, Commissioner Cecil Bowers on fiddle, and commission employees Oscar Coates and Roy Gainey playing guitars and harmonizing on the songs. The music ranged far and wide, from Jimmy Rodgers's blue yodels to Merle Haggard, from Baptist hymns to "Danny Boy" and anything country-modern that was in the air. Local and not-so-local talent showed up and took the mike, and once in a while they even sang their favorite song. Kurt Vonnegut once croaked out "Red River Valley," and over the years John Irving, Tom Wolfe, Pat Conroy, Garrison Keillor, James Dickey, Nora Ephron, Pauline Kael, Stephen Spender, John Gardner, and Bruce Springsteen all took the mike and said, "Hello, I'm sure glad to be here."

The high point of the Tuesday nights here was the wild and woolly rendition of "Orange Blossom Special," with Cecil smoking on his fiddle and congressmen and the local citizens heel-and-toe clogging in the aisles, yipping out enough yeeeee-haaaaws to keep the beer glasses rattling. After the reverberations died down—it took a while—a hush came over the room as Oscar Coates chorded his guitar and let the sound hang in the air. Then he'd lean in on the microphone: "OK. Now remember. No dancing during gospel." And he'd segue into "I'll Fly Away," singing with an intensity of feeling that brought tears to the eyes of the faithful and was absolutely beyond description. Ahh, the passing of the good old days at the Capitol.

by the Bluegrass Jammin' at 9 p.m. every Fri. Legends Country Night begins at 7 p.m. (doors open at 6 p.m.); check their calendar for Sat event dates. Admission is $15 at the door, and it's worth every penny. Once in a while, for special occasions, the admission is a covered dish. If you decide to bring one, don't show up with any alcohol—it's not allowed here. Check out bills musicshop.com or call (803) 796-6477.

At 116 State St., West Columbia, you can find a row of restaurants (sometimes referred to as the West Vista), including the very quaint and very cool **@116 State Espresso & Wine Bar.** It has outdoor seating, and the atmosphere is straight comfort. On any given day you will find high school students mixed with college students mixed with business executives, all talking to each other and enjoying the wide range of espressos and delicious food. While you're there, you may want to have one of their "house specials," which would consist of any number of different creations concocted by owner and chef Ryan Whitaker from locally sourced fish, meats, and produce. They also have an interesting coffee menu, with one of the leading sellers being the Almond Chocolate Coffee, a gourmet coffee steamed with amaretto and crème de cacao, topped with whipped cream and chocolate shavings. Along with a nice selection of vino, they have a White Russian menu featuring the classic drink as well as one called the Colorado Bulldog and a Pumpkin Spiced Espresso White Russian. Some of the food has a Spanish flair, such as paella and the *huevos rellenos.* The empanada of the day gets rave reviews. Prices are good here—the small tapas plates run around $7 or $8, with the large plates a little more. Not bad! Hours are 4 to 10 p.m. Tues through Thurs and 4 p.m. to midnight Fri and Sat. Brunch is served from 10 a.m. to 3 p.m. on Sat and Sun. Call (803) 791-5663 or visit 116state.com.

On the same street, at 100 State St., is **Terra,** a very upscale, uptown restaurant. Reservations are recommended, and they have valet parking! The updated Southern-style menu changes daily with seasonal offerings and will run you anywhere from $6 to $12—if you order one of the delicious appetizers—to around $30 for an entree with wine. Some of their locally sourced menu items have included Grilled Fudge Farms Pork Porterhouse, with braised Napa cabbage, garlic sausage, roasted apple sauce, and mustard bourbon jus; and Seared Sea Scallops, with sweet corn and butter bean succotash, bacon, mushrooms, and sherry mustard butter. You'll feel as if you are in another city while eating here; it is dark and romantic, yet cosmopolitan and usually very crowded, and always fun. Wednesdays find the wood oven especially busy with their popular Pizza & Pinot specials. This is an exciting restaurant owned by chef Mike Davis, a James Beard House invitee, among his other numerous notable culinary accolades. Open Tues through Sat at 5 p.m.; closed Sun and Mon. Call (803) 791-3443 or visit terrasc.com.

Home of the finest mustard-based, sauce-drenched barbecue in the Southeast, **Piggie Park** is so famous that its product is shipped to every state in the country and all over the world. Almost as famous is Maurice Bessinger, the owner and operator. During the 1950s he was an ardent segregationist, but in the 1960s he found Jesus and became a leading integrationist. Next he ran for governor on a white horse and lost, and then, discovering something in Scripture, he turned his Barbecue Buffeteria into a mission for the gospel.

Maurice can't seem to stay out of trouble and the public eye. At one time he would not remove his Confederate flag from the top of his restaurant, but negotiations resulted in his lowering it under the Stars and Stripes and the State Palmetto Flag. Despite this, stop in here anyway. The food is excellent, and you don't have to load up on religious tracts or listen to Maurice if you don't want to. But if you're lucky, he'll stop by your table and tell you a lot more than you're willing to listen to about the old Confederacy.

A Few More Words about Barbecue

For some reason, rednecks down here in the "hard lard belt" are now billing their barbecue as "gourmet barbecue." But it's a free country, and you can call it anything you want. Anyhow, there are a few not-so-well-known facts I thought I'd pass along to the tourists and the transplants to raise their sensitivity and make them much better consumers.

Basically there are three classifications for barbecue hogs: the three rib down, the five rib down, and the seven rib down. This is the butcher's term that tells you how much a rack of ribs weighs. What this also tells you is the three rib down comes from a smaller hog that has less fat than the five rib, and considerably less than the seven rib down hog. The result of all this is that the three rib down is smaller and thinner and has less fat and is obviously tastier. As a result, three rib down is much more expensive, harder to find, and is really the only truly "gourmet barbecue." A basic rule would be that a buffet of "All You Can Eat Barbecue" that has to withstand the seismic charge of entire football teams will probably be five rib down. Meanwhile, out at the fair and political fund-raising functions where the beer drinkers will eat anything, there is a strong chance it'll be the fatter seven rib down.

I guess it all boils down to this: The next time someone tells you about "gourmet barbecue," ask what kind of hogs he or she uses. They will say, "What do you mean?" And you answer, "Well, judging by the length and weight of this here rib and all this fat dripping on my leisure suit . . ."

Maurice practices what he preaches: good food at a reasonable price and an unswerving belief in every word of the Scriptures. Eat one of his "Little Joe" barbecue sandwiches with a side of the best onion rings you'll ever find.

Back when Al McGuire coached Marquette and they came to town to play USC's Gamecocks, his first stop in town was Maurice's. Joseph Heller, author of *Catch 22,* loved it. So did the late Nora Ephron, who directed *Sleepless in Seattle,* and so did Mickey Spillane, who lived down the road in Murrells Inlet. During Desert Storm, the 240th Combat Communications Squadron from nearby McEntire Air Base asked Maurice to send some barbecue to Kuwait. Maurice couldn't fill that order, but when the 200 men returned to Columbia, he gave them and their spouses a free all-they-could-eat barbecue meal at the base. Most locations are open daily 10 a.m. to 10 p.m. The main store is at 1600 Charleston Hwy. Call (803) 791-5887 or visit mauricesbbq.com for the location nearest you.

To reach **Lexington Arms** from downtown Columbia, take Highway 1 14 miles south to 314 W. Main St., Lexington. Around here Highway 1 is called the Two Notch Road until it gets out of town, then it changes to US 1 and goes on about its business as it runs on up the road to Maine. It begins at the first phone pole in Florida down at Key West. Anyway, this is the home of Elizabeth and Duncan Crowe and their five children and probably the best and most varied menu in the Carolinas and Georgia.

At age 15, in the famous Swiss hotel school, La Ron, Elizabeth was one of the few women enrolled, but while the others wanted to be dietitians, she began her career as a chef. Today, she says, despite the hard work and long hours, some of her happiest moments were at La Ron, where she learned the fine art of German and French cuisine. "I still remember those chefs dressed in white with their silver spoons around their necks." When she finished school, she had planned to return to her home in Heidelburg to help her mother open a cafe, but being independent, she followed a different course. "I ran away. My mother always had big plans of opening a hotel and dining club. She was going to be the boss and I was going to do all the work. In Europe, women in the kitchen were usually paid lower wages and often forced to give away their cooking secrets. With my papers from La Ron, I knew I could always get work in America, or, for that matter, anywhere."

Elizabeth's husband, Duncan, whom she met in Kansas City, where she was manager of the Riverboat Restaurant, was born in London and began his career in the wine trade, working as a wine salesman. He went to the West Indies in the hotel business and then transferred to Kansas City. After their marriage, Elizabeth and Duncan operated a resort hotel in Antigua and lived and worked in Florida before coming to Lexington and purchasing the Lexington Arms.

Elizabeth says she and Duncan have "some sort of aversion to big cities that developed when we lived on the island. It was small. Everybody knew everybody. That's why we are so happy here in Lexington." Duncan added that they wanted to establish the same kind of familiar atmosphere at the Lexington Arms. "We want it to develop into a community area, a cafe setting. We want people to feel it's their restaurant, whether they want a full meal or just a cup of coffee or a glass of beer. As a matter of fact, if you sit at the bar and decide to have a full meal there, that's fine with us."

From the outside, the Lexington Arms looks like a British pub. But Elizabeth and Duncan have taken great care to brighten up the interior and have made it casual and comfortable and a great place just to come in for a beer. The combination of Elizabeth's German, French, and Swiss cuisine and Duncan's British background has resulted in exactly what they wanted—a first-class restaurant that specializes in German, French, and Swiss cuisine, with, of course, many standard American entrees and Caribbean dishes, as well as a very fine and complete wine list.

The wine bar allows you to order some of the finest wines by the glass—the perfect way to try something new. Elizabeth and Duncan's sons, Charles and Phillip, both now chefs, help out in the kitchen, so the Crowe dynasty is in very good shape for many, many years to come. Hours are 5:30 to 9 p.m. Tues through Thurs and 5:30 to 10 p.m. Fri and Sat. Closed Sun and Mon. German dishes are served only on Thurs and Sat, and French dishes only on Tues and Wed. The lounge opens at 4 p.m. and happy hour runs until 7 p.m. Call (803) 359-2700 or visit lexingtonarms.net.

Richard Riley, former governor of South Carolina and secretary of education, once waved his arms and pronounced that Rhoten's sausage featured at ***Rhoten's Country Store*** at 720 E. Main St. was the best of the best in the Palmetto State. Since that time there have been a few small changes: First, the original Rhoten's General Store went out of business; second, it became a mattress store, stacked to the ceiling and window levels with full-, queen-, and king-size mattresses. But the old ways die hard around here, and the populace insisted that they continue selling their pork sausage, which they did. The result was the only store in the Western world that sold mattresses and pork sausage, and only mattresses and pork sausage, giving new meaning to the term "bed and breakfast"! Everyone said the mattresses were good, but not quite as good as the sausage, so today the mattresses are gone and the sausage is back in a country store setting. Rhoten's has local arts and crafts, gift items, homemade jams and jellies, and lots of interesting bric-a-brac. So when you come through Lexington, stop on in, and if you get here in the cool months, you can load up on pork sausage. Hours at Rhoten's are 10 a.m. to 6 p.m. Tues through Sat. Call (803) 359-6219.

Inside the *Flight Deck Restaurant* in downtown Lexington at 109A Old Chapin Rd., there is something you simply cannot leave South Carolina without seeing—a 15-foot plastic cast of mighty King Kong straddling the Empire State Building. With his right hand he is holding on to the antenna on top of the building and glowering at the attacking planes that will eventually be his undoing, while with his left he is crushing a 6-foot model of a Stearman biplane. Your kids will be talking about this forever. Meanwhile, if there is any red blood in your system, you will be absolutely awestruck by the collection of incredible model planes that cover the ceiling, the foyers, and every inch of wall space. Now, I'm not talking about handheld models you wind up with rubber bands and fly across a room or down a hallway. I'm talking about a P-47 Thunderbolt with a 12-foot wingspan, an enormous P-51, huge B-17s, 24s, 29s, and modern jet fighters. The range is incredible and only a madman or someone like Ted Stambolitis, who owns and operates the place, would have dared do all this by himself. Yes, he built the planes, hung them, and knows every inch of each of them. And he will be delighted to show you around and answer any and all questions. Incidentally, Ted, also a licensed pilot, has actually flown everything from hang gliders to experimental aircraft.

But more than just a museum of old planes, the Flight Deck is a busy, very successful restaurant specializing in sandwiches, blue plate special meals, and home-baked cookies and desserts. Everything here is first-rate, moderately priced, and exceptionally clean. It's an ideal place to bring, and maybe even leave, the kids. Hours are Mon through Thurs 11 a.m. to 9 p.m., Fri and Sat 11 a.m. to 10 p.m. Closed Sun. Call (803) 957-5990. You can see more of the ambiance at flightdeckrestaurant.net.

A Little Fish Tail . . . er, Tale

OK, a little stroll down memory lane. On the corner of Huger and Gervais, right across from the old brick building now housing a Publix grocery store, was a wrought-iron window. Back in the 1940s and 1950s, my grandmother Fanny— Dad's mother—did a lively business in this tiny spot selling fish sandwiches and fish sandwiches only. First she would buy the fish from the folks fishing the river two blocks away. Then she would clean them and fry them in 450-degree lard and serve them between two slices of bread in a wax wrapper with a pickle chip on top for a dime. The customers would bring their own soft drinks and sit on the Gervais Street curb watching the Fords and Chevys go by, or on the Huger Street side looking down at the river. The fish sandwich was served with the head and tail intact, and most of the customers ate everything except the long spinal column. Now, talk about fine dining! Anyhow, Grandma did a lively business right here.

One of the most enjoyable things I did while researching this book was walk in the ***Francis Beidler Forest*** at Four Holes Swamp in Harleyville. To get there from Columbia, take I-26 south to exit 177, turning right on Highway 453 to Highway 178 through Harleyville, and follow the signs to the forest. A 1.75-mile boardwalk takes you through the largest remaining virgin stand of bald cypress and tupelo gum trees in the world. It is truly awesome. Many of these forest giants rising out of the clear pools and black-water streams are 1,000 years old, or older, and reach up well over 200 feet. Alligators, snakes, and every conceivable native animal can be seen if you are quiet and stand still. In the evenings you can even see owls and an occasional otter. A self-guiding tour booklet leads you through this natural cathedral in the forest. It's a walk you will never, ever forget.

The forest is named for the lumberman-conservationist Francis Beidler, who preserved the area from logging. Unconventional for a lumberman of his time, he allowed much of his timber to stand while taxes, interest, hurricanes, and insects took their toll. After his death in 1924, his family and later the National Audubon Society and the Nature Conservancy raised the money to continue his program and even expand the sanctuary. Today it covers more than 16,000 spectacular acres. If I had one place to visit in South Carolina and only one, I'd go here. Open to the public from 9 a.m. to 5 p.m. Tues through Sun. Closed Mon and on Thanksgiving; December

Back Roads You Don't Want to Be Out on Too Late at Night

Coming out of Harleyville is a two-lane blacktop winding through a part of the old Palmetto State that may never change. IMPEACH EARL WARREN has faded badly on the smooth rocks and runoff culverts, but GET US OUT OF THE UN . . . is still with us in fresh spray paint, along with directions for where to buy night crawlers, crickets, and she-crab soup, and where you can get a good head, palm, or root reading. One sign in tortured hand lettering outside Bluffton—the area that gave the world Father Devine, Reverend Ike, and more recently Del Webb—looks as if it has been lifted from *The Guinness Book of World Records:* MAN HAS GOTTEN AWAY WITH MORE SIN AND UNRIGHTEOUSNESS DURING THE PAST TWENTY YEARS THAN DURING ANY PERIOD SINCE GOD DROVE ADAM AND EVE FROM THE GARDEN OF EDEN.

24, 25, and 31; and January 1. Admission for adults is $8, children 6 to 12 pay $4, children younger than 6 are admitted free, and discounts apply for Audubon members. Call (843) 462-2150 or write Sanctuary Manager, Francis Beidler Forest, 336 Sanctuary Rd., Harleyville 29448. Their website is beidler forest.audubon.org. That's, as they say, a wrap.

Places to Stay in Uplands & Columbia

COLUMBIA

Chestnut Cottage B&B
1718 Hampton St.
(803) 256-1718
chestnutcottage.com

The 1425 Inn
1425 Richland St.
(803) 252-7225
the1425inn.com

EDGEFIELD

Pleasant Lane Acres B&B
318 Pleasant Ln.
(803) 637-9387
pleasantlaneacres.com

GREENVILLE

Park House B&B
221 E. Park Ave.
(864) 232-2020
parkhousebedand
breakfast.com

Pettigru Place B&B
302 Pettigru St.
(864) 242-4529
pettigruplace.com

LANDRUM

Country Mouse Inn
120 N. Trade Ave.
(864) 457-4061
theinnkeeper.com/
bnb/11000

Red Horse Inn
45 Winstons Chase Ct.
(864) 895-4968
theredhorseinn.com

ROCK HILL

Book & Spindle
626 Oakland Ave.
(803) 328-1913

East Main Guest House
600 E. Main St.
(803) 366-1161
eastmainsc.com

SALEM

**Sunrise Farm Bed &
Breakfast**
325 Sunrise Dr.
(864) 944-0121
sunrisefarmbb.com

SPARTANBURG

Walnut Lane Inn B&B
110 Ridge Rd., Lyman
(864) 949-7230
walnutlaneinn.com

UNION

Inn at Merridun
100 Merridun Place
(864) 427-7052
merridun.com

Nicholson Mansion B&B
2403 Crosskeys Hwy.
(864) 424-9042
nicholsonmansion.com

Places to Eat in Uplands & Columbia

BUFFALO

Midway Barbecue
811 Main St.
(864) 427-4047

COLUMBIA

Dianne's on Devine
2400 Devine St.
(803) 254-3535
diannesondevine.com

Garibaldi's
2013 Greene St.
(803) 771-8888
garibaldicolumbia.com

**Goatfeathers Coffee Bar
& Restaurant**
2017 Devine St.
(803) 256-3325

Longhorn Steakhouse
902 Gervais St., Ste. A
(803) 254-5100
longhornsteakhouse.com

Motor Supply Company
920 Gervais St.
(803) 256-6687
motorsupplycobistro.com

Za's Brick Oven Pizza
2930 Devine St.
(803) 771-7334
zasbrickovenpizza.com

GREENVILLE

**Beano Brothers Coffee
and Cafe**
4 Independence Pointe
(864) 675-0303

Cafe and Then Some
101 College St.
(864) 232-2287
cafeats.com

Chophouse 47
36 Beacon Dr.
(864) 287-8700
chophouse47.com

Travinia Italian Kitchen
1625 Woodruff Rd.
(864) 458-8188
travinia.com

SPARTANBURG

The Flounder
160 Barbado Ln.
(864) 576-3165

Gerhard's Cafe
1200 E. Main St.
(864) 591-1920
gerhardscafe.net

Index